Love Unlimited

LOVE UNLIMITED

KING JESUS PRESS LLC

Love Unlimited

LOVE UNLIMITED

Damone Paul Johnson

Love Unlimited

Copyright ©2025 by Damone Paul Johnson,
Albany, New York www.damonepauljohnson.com

All rights reserved. Except as permitted under the U.S. Copyright Act of 1976, no part of this publication may be reproduced, distributed or transmitted in any form or by any means, or stored in a database or retrieval system, without the prior written permission of the publisher.

ISBN: 978-1-7368046-2-9 (Soft cover)
ISBN: 978-1-7368046-1-2 (E-book)

Unless otherwise indicated, Scripture verses quoted are from the King James Version of the Bible, public domain.

Scripture quotations are taken from the New King James Version®. Copyright © 1982 by Thomas Nelson. Used by permission. All rights reserved.

THE HOLY BIBLE, NEW INTERNATIONAL VERSION®, NIV® Copyright © 1973, 1978, 1984, 2011 by Biblica, Inc.® Used by permission. All rights reserved worldwide.

Scripture quotations marked (NLT) are taken from the Holy Bible, New Living Translation, copyright ©1996, 2004, 2007, 2013, 2015 by Tyndale House Foundation. Used by permission of Tyndale House Publishers, Inc., Carol Stream, Illinois 60188. All rights reserved.

PRAISE FOR LOVE UNLIMITED

If you are searching for a book that not only deepens your understanding of love, but also challenges you to live it out daily, "Love Unlimited" by Dr. Damone Johnson is a must-read. Rooted in the timeless truths of 1 Corinthians 13, this book offers a powerful, practical, and spiritually-grounded look at what it truly means to love God's way. Dr. Johnson unpacks this chapter with clarity and conviction, helping the readers move beyond surface emotions to the sacrificial, patient, enduring love that the Scripture calls you to embody. Whether you are navigating relationships, marriage, ministry, or personal growth, "Love Unlimited" offers insight and encouragement that will inspire you to love more intentionally, just as Christ loves us. This book is transformational. Dr. Johnson doesn't just describe love. He equips you to love.

Dr. Addis Moore
National Baptist Convention, USA Inc.
Congress of Christian Education – Dean of Academic Affairs

Dr. Johnson takes care to breakdown love in a way that's powerful, profound and practical. Each page exposes love as God originally intended and empowers us to live it out daily.

Rev. Dr. Shanell Turnpin
Pastor - Second Baptist Church, Catskill, NY

Does love come naturally or is it a learned behavior? I believe it is the latter, and to that end there is no better way to learn how to love than through the example of Jesus. I appreciate Dr. Johnson's attention to detail as he breaks down every aspect of God's love as it is presented in the Bible. May the love of Christ abide in us all as we learn about LOVE UNLIMITED.

Rev. Dr. Nikki D. Jean-Simon

Love Unlimited

"Love Unlimited" is more than a book. It is an invitation to live a life transformed by the power of God's love. Rooted in the timeless truths of 1 Corinthians 13, this work thoughtfully unpacks what it means to love with patience, kindness, humility, and grace in a world that desperately needs it. With biblical depth and personal insight, the author challenges us not just to feel love but to live it. As you read this book, allow the Holy Spirit to shape you into someone who loves…like this.

Rev. Dr. Elgin Joseph Taylor, Sr.
Senior Pastor, Sweet Pilgrim Missionary Baptist Church

Dr. Johnson's latest book, "Love Unlimited," is devoted to the importance of love and how we all desire to love and be loved, no matter who we are. It is a follow up from his 2022 book, "Bonded Love," which focused on relationships. I believe this new book is going to help readers love themselves, and then give them tools on how to love others. I love how he uses 1 Corinthians to demonstrate the freedom of love and underlines the importance of showing kindness; not to get something in return, but to give.

Rev. Constance Knight
Pastor - Welcome Chapel Missionary Baptist Church, Albany, NY

This book will reveal to you that love is an art. Damone Paul Johnson creatively explores the deeper nuances of love's limitless capabilities, using imagery that sparks the imagination. He teaches timeless principles rooted in action. Inspiring and honest.

Dr. Shai Butler
Author & Speaker - "Better. Not Perfect: From Hot Mess to Life Success"

DEDICATION

To My Queen,

I love you not because of what I am, but because of who I am when I'm with you. I love you because you took the side road of my life and with love, patience and respect, made it a highway of promise and purpose.

Love Unlimited

CONTENTS

Foreword..xi

Introduction..xiii

Chapter 1 - Love Is Patient......................................1

Chapter 2 - Love Is Kind..7

Chapter 3 - Love Does Not Envy...........................13

Chapter 4 - Love Is Not Full of Pride.....................21

Chapter 5 - Love Is Not Rude.................................31

Chapter 6 - Love Is Courteous................................39

Chapter 7 - Love Is Not Selfish..............................49

Chapter 8 - Walking In the Spirit of Love..............59

Chapter 9 - Love Never Fails.................................67

Chapter 10 - I'm Growing Up.................................77

Chapter 11 - Personal Spiritual Journey on Love...87

Acknowledgments...97

About the Author..99

Love Unlimited

x

FOREWORD

In a world that so often confuses love with performance, transaction, or spectacle, "Love Unlimited" calls us back to love's original source – God. This is not the shallow, self-indulgent love paraded across screens and social media feeds. This is love as defined by 1 Corinthians 13 as radical and resilient. Love that suffers long and is kind. Love that endures. Love that convicts. Love that liberates. Dr. Damone Johnson offers a theologically grounded, biblically faithful, and pastorally relevant exploration of love, not as mere sentiment, but as divine imperative and transformative power.

"Love Unlimited" invites the reader on a journey, not merely to *learn* about love, but to be *shaped* by it. We are challenged to recognize the ways love has shaped (and sometimes misshaped) our own identities. Readers will be asked to reflect on how freely we should extend grace, kindness, patience and hope. But more than anything, we are pointed toward the One whose love is the beautiful, transformative blueprint for it all.

Dr. Johnson rightly situates love as eternal, unlimited and free, a claim that is both doctrine and disruptive. It challenges us to move beyond transactional forms of affection and embrace a divine love that is active, liberative and communal. He draws on scriptural exposition, theological reflection, and cultural illustration to render love both comprehensible and convicting. His use of metaphor, comparing love to the arts, invites the reader to approach love not merely as ethic, but as aesthetic and spiritual practices.

Dr. Johnson does not write from a place of detached scholarship. He writes from the pulpit and the prayer closet, from lived experience and Spirit-led insight and revelation. His words will comfort, confront, and ultimately call us to love deeper, wider, and more faithfully.

This is not a book to skim. It is a book to sit with. Read it with your Bible open. Read it with your journal nearby. Read it with an open heart ready to reimagine what love can look like when God is in the center. Love still has the power to heal what's broken, restore what's been lost, and renew what's been overlooked.

Rev. Nicole Patrice Guns, M. Div.
Senior Pastor, First Baptist Church of Gary
Gary, Indiana

INTRODUCTION

Love is one of the most desired attributes in the human experience. We long to feel the euphoria of encountering love and spend a considerable amount of time trying to understand what it is. This book helps break it down.

Since the beginning of time, we have been wrestling with the identity of love. If you look throughout history from generation to generation, comprehending the word *love* has been a constant evolution. Is love euphoric? Can love be truly identified? Are we chasing another fleeting thought that man has placed on life's hamster wheel? As you begin to ponder these questions, prayerfully, this book will reveal many answers on love.

Let us explore what love is in its most basic form. When you break it down, you will find three components of love: love being unlimited, love being eternal, and love being free. As you read this book, you will learn that love is limitless. Even if you put your ideas of love into categories, the way love is given and received is truly endless. For some, you may feel love when someone looks at you with a warm glow in their eyes in the most attentive and adoring way. For others, you may feel love if someone gifts you a brand new, top-of-the-line Mercedes Benz. Either scenario could equally be an ultimate sign of love for the receiver, depending on their perspective. This example gives you a visual perspective of love, but love goes far beyond feelings. It is how you communicate, how you think, how you respond, and even how you believe.

Love Unlimited

I published a book in 2022 titled, "Bonded Love: How God's Love Shines Through Imperfect Relationships." "Love Unlimited" is a continuation of this topic on love. Since love is the foundation of the greatest commandment, it is worth exploring it further. This book demonstrates how love is eternal. Love is before the beginning to never an ending. Yes, love is always. I know it would be extremely easy to write about how love existed from the beginning of time, and that would be a factual statement because God is love, and He was before time. However, we will delve into the complexity or simplicity of love from the beginning of *your* time. Your concept and understanding of love today result from how you were loved as an infant. Before you could walk, talk, or even hold your head up for yourself, you were already recognizing and absorbing the concept of love. You will see as you read this book how you can recognize your love profile and how you can use God's word to enhance or even change it.

Throughout this book, you will begin to have a greater understanding of the unlimited capabilities of love and appreciate the eternalness of love. Now I hope you know this could not be a book about love if I did not give you the space to explore and value how free love is. As we investigate the 15 verbs of love found in 1 Corinthians 13, it will become very clear why love is free. At times you may find love to be challenging. You may even find love to be testing, but it never comes with a cost. Could you imagine a life where love is totally personal, but yet totally communal? What if every day you wake up with the confidence of knowing you are loved to your expectations and desires, simply because the love you aspire to have already is in and around you? Is that the happiness you are searching for? Even better, how elated would you be if your attempts to share your love with others were received the same way you intended the person to receive it? Get ready to understand the freeness of love!

Okay, have I piqued your interest about love enough for you to want to read further? Well before you dive into chapter one, let us first clarify what this book is not. If you are looking for a self-help book to immediately fix a spiraling love situation, although this book may be helpful, it is probably not your go-to book. However, if you are seeking a greater understanding of love from the Source, I know you have found your book.

In the New Testament of the Bible, God allowed the Apostle Paul to write the descriptive actions of love in 1 Corinthians. It was in the 13th chapter that he gave Paul 15 verbs to help us identify what we view as love today. For the last few years, God has given me the assignment to research and explore those same 15 verbs to bestow upon the readers a more comprehensible perception of love. This book will reveal to you that love is an art. Like music, love can be loud, rhythmic and harmonic. As you traverse through these chapters, you will begin to see love as a whole orchestra where you are the conductor. But, you will not only identify love as music, you will see it as a theater or a stage play as well. You will begin to understand how love can appear so seamless from afar, but realize the effort and work it takes for people to embrace one another's idea of love.

Lastly, you will see love as a piece of painted art. Art is valued by the artist who places the paint on the canvas. A three-year-old toddler can make five brush strokes on a canvas, and before the night is over, the canvas may reach the garbage can. Now a trained, known artist can pick up the same size canvas and make the same five brush strokes. That piece can become a priceless work of art. Why? What makes the difference? One word – inspiration. This book is going to allow you to understand that the world around you is your canvas, the 15 verbs we are about to dive into are your brushes, and the relationship you develop with the source of love - GOD - will bring the inspiration behind your idea of love, so that everyone you encounter will feel the presence and value of it. Let's get started.

Chapter 1

LOVE IS PATIENT
1 Corinthians 13:4 NIV

"Love is patient..."

The Apostle Paul writes about love in 1 Corinthians 13 to the entire church. There is a need for all of us to have and demonstrate godly love – agape love. Love is desiring the best for someone. There is a need for it because unfortunately, some people in the church believe if they have gifts, skills and abilities, they do not need love. But Paul shows us that if you have all of those attributes – generous hearts, possess great gifts, and possess great goodness – but don't have love, you are just making noise. If you possess great goodness, but don't have love, that goodness means nothing.

Nature of Love

Paul gives 15 verbs between verses 4-9 to describe what love is. Love is an action. It is not just what you think or say, it is what you do. Don't tell me you love me and don't do something. The first thing he says is love is patient. Patience is not just waiting. Even though we should wait and love is long suffering, it is deeper than that. This type of love is the type that restricts retaliation when someone wrongs you. In 2 Peter 3:9 it talks about how God is not slack concerning His love because he desires that none of us be destroyed but all will come into a time of repentance. God is a God of patience. Think about it. How many times have you let God down? How many times have you disobeyed God? How many times have you missed the mark with God, yet He continues

Love Unlimited

to love you, give to you, and show you grace and mercy? The patience of God is reflected in the fact that we are still here. It is shown to this nation, this world, and to you. Patience is when someone wrongs and offends you, but you do not strike back.

David knew he was anointed by God to be the next king. Saul, who was the king, tried to kill David on 22 different occasions because of his insecurity. When David was on the run, he had the opportunity to kill Saul, but he did not do it. There were times when Saul was vulnerable. What did David do? He did not strike back because he had the love of patience. This patience is long suffering, and long suffering is not just enduring. It is not striking back even when someone wrongs you.

If you really want to know how that is demonstrated, look at Jesus on the cross. They jeered Him. They mocked Him. They beat Him. He was forced to carry His own cross, then they put Him on it with 6-inch nails in his hands and 9-foot spikes in His feet, and a crown of thorns on His head to tease Him about being King of the Jews. As they were jeering Him and mocking Him, they put a sword in His side. As they were down their laughing at Him, Jesus could have called legions of angels to wipe all of them out. But, the first thing He said on the cross was, *"Father, forgive them. For they know not what they do."* Jesus shows us a lot about this long suffering – this patient type of love. He shows us that love restrains itself, even while still being hurt. Even while they were mocking Him. Even while they were laughing at Him. Instead of lashing back. He said, *"Father, forgive them."*

Now, let me back up. When I say *while still being hurt*, I don't mean stay in a relationship where you are being physically abused. It is not God's will for anybody to put their hands on you.

Love Unlimited

And if you are in that type of relationship, that is not love, and you need to find a way to get out of there. I know it may not be easy, especially if children are involved, but that is not God's will for you to stay in that relationship or marriage where you are physically being assaulted.

Even though love does not retaliate, love restrains itself while it is still hurting. Some people say, *"I'll forgive Him when it no longer hurts me."* Or, *"I'll forgive Him when I'm finished with it emotionally."* No, you ought to forgive while you still have the pain.

For some people, you may have a strained relationship with your mother or father. Every relationship between parent and child is not warm and fuzzy. Some of you may not have had the best mother or father and struggle with it even today. But, love forgives – refuses to retaliate – even while you are still hurting.

Jesus shows us that love restrains itself, even while you still see the one who offended you. They say, *"Out of sight, out of mind,"* but what do you do when you still have to look at the person? It would be easy to forgive if you did not work at the same job, were not in the same class, did not go to the same school, or were not at the same church. It would be easy to forgive if you did not live in the same house. If you did not sleep in the same bed.

Even while you see them, love refuses to retaliate. *"Father, forgive them."* While you are still looking at them. While you can still see them. Jesus did not say, *"Father, get them! Take them out!"* He could have. But he said, *"Father, forgive them."*

Love Unlimited

Love restrains itself and forgives, even when the person who offended you does not apologize. Now, I have to admit, I struggle with this one. Because if you do something to me and you apologize, I can let it go. I promise you I can let it go and will not bring it up again. But when you know you wronged me, then act like everything is okay, and you expect me to just get amnesia and forget about what you did, that does not work for me! If we did a DNA analysis on the knife you put in my back, there is a 99.9 percent chance your fingerprints are on it. But, you do not say anything; acting like everything is ok. I struggle with that! However, love restrains itself and forgives, even if the offender has not apologized.

You want to forgive because forgiveness frees you. I will be the first one to say it is not easy. But, I do not think it is by accident – when Paul lists these 15 verbs in 1 Corinthians 13 – that patience is the first one listed. While you are mad and angry at the one who offended you, while your blood pressure is going up, while your heart is racing and you are tossing and turning, while you are cussing and fussing, the person you are mad at is going on about their business, not even thinking about you.

For some of you, you have had issues with relationships in the past, but you cannot see what God is showing you in the present and the future because you have not dealt with it. If you do not deal with it, it will creep up in future relationships. You have to let that go because unforgiveness straps you and keeps you bound. If you want to know how to do that, look at Jesus as the example. He said, *"Father, forgive them for they know not what they do."* If they had known Jesus was the Messiah, if they really understood that He was the Christ and the Anointed One, they would have never done that. Same as that person who offended you. If they really understood what that was going to do. When that parent or loved one walked out on you. But, if they really understood how that would have impacted you and shaped your world view, they would have not done that.

"Father, forgive them, for they know not what they do." You can read this sentence two different ways. When they put Jesus on the cross, they thought they were stopping something. They did not realize they were pushing Jesus further to His purpose. He came to die. He was the Lamb of God that was slain before the foundation of the world. They did not realize they were in the will of God and was part of a plan God made before the beginning of the world. *"Father, forgive them for they know not what they do."*

When that job let you go, they thought they were stopping something, but they did not realize they were birthing a business. They did not realize they were starting a new bachelor's or master's degree. When that person dogged you, they thought they were stopping something, but did not realize they were starting a new self-esteem. They did not realize they were starting a new mentality. They did not realize they were starting a mindset that says, *"I will never be treated like that by anyone else."* They did not realize what they were doing. *"Father, forgive them for they know not what they do."* They don't know, but there is coming a day when they will know!

The Bible tells us that every knee shall bow and every tongue shall confess that He is King of Kings and LORD OF LORDS. They will know that He is the Great I am. They will know that no weapon formed against you shall prosper. And every tongue that shall rise against thee in judgment though shalt condemn. They will know that greater is He that is in you than he that is in the world!

Love Unlimited

Let us pray: LORD, we thank you for your love. We thank you for your patience and long suffering. Now LORD, there is a mechanism in our flesh that desires to get even and retaliate. Help us to understand that you said vengeance is yours and you will repay. Although we are not to be anyone's doormat, we are to exercise divine love. Help us to do that as you have shown us on the cross. For those who are struggling with relationships with parents, spouses, ex's, or friends, we pray you give us a heart of forgiveness and love because it frees us. So many people are bound with anger, bitterness and hatred. Help us to walk in divine love today. Thank you that you so loved us that you gave your only begotten Son. In Jesus' name, we say Hallelujah and amen.

Chapter 2

LOVE IS KIND
1 Corinthians 13:4a NKJV

"Love suffers long and is kind..."

There are two qualities or attributes of God - His mercy and His grace. Mercy is when God holds back what *we do* deserve. We commit some type of infraction, and He withholds His punishment from us. The prophet Jeremiah said it is because of His mercy that we are not consumed. Grace is what God extends to us that we *do not* deserve.

The Distinction of Love Through Kindness

Those are not just qualities from the LORD. Those are qualities God expects from us. Those who are blood-bought believers and children of the LORD are called to love. The love that the Apostle Paul describes to us has many sides to it like a kaleidoscope. It is multi-faceted, almost like a diamond. He gives us another phase, color or type of love. He said love is kind. In the first chapter, you learned about how love is patient, which means we hold back on the revenge we want to give someone. Because God said, *"Vengeance is mine. I will repay."* But there is another side to it. Not only do we hold revenge, but God expects us to extend kindness. Even to the one who dogged us out. This is what he means by kindness.

Love suffers long *and* (a connective conjunction) is kind. They go together. They are two sides of the same coin. Notice the distinction of love through kindness. It is not just, *"You dogged*

me and I can get you back," but, *"I am not going to do it."* That is one level. That could just mean you have resolve. You are tough and can withstand something. God said take it to another level. Don't just not get back. Can you turn around and be kind to the one who is doing you wrong? Paul said in Romans 12, *"If your enemy is hungry, feed him. If he is thirsty, give him a drink; for in so doing you will heap coals of fire on his head."* It is one thing for me to withhold, but it is another thing to extend that type of kindness. *You mean extend kindness to the one who did me wrong? You mean to the one who has been dogging me out?* Jesus said, *"Bless those who curse you. Pray for those who despitefully use you."* Now, that does not mean you are a doormat. It does not mean allow someone to make a fool out of you. Jesus also said, *"Be wise as a serpent and harmless as a dove."*

The Description of Love Through Kindness

God is calling us to extend love and kindness to those without expecting anything in return. Can you give without it being, *"You scratch my back and I scratch yours?"* This takes it to another level. Can you extend kindness and love to someone without expecting something back? It is one thing to be kind to you because I have an ulterior motive – *let me do you a favor because down the road, I will call you for a favor.* But the God-kind of love says *I am giving to you, not because I want something, but because it is the right thing to do.*

There is a story about Mother Teresa who used to take care of lepers in Calcutta. A group of tourists went to this leper colony because they wanted to see Mother Teresa. When they found her, she was bandaging a leper's wound that did not look pretty. One of the tourists observed this and grunted, *"I wouldn't do that for a million dollars!"* Without looking up, Mother Theresa said, *"I wouldn't either. That is not why I am doing this."* The love of God is extended to those who are not in position to give something back to you.

The Demonstration of Love Through Kindness

The demonstration of this type of love is the divine nature of kindness. In fact, the evidence of God's kindness to us is that God extended love to us, and we were not in position to give back to Him. While we were yet sinners, Christ died for us. Romans 2:4 says, *"Or do you despise the riches of His goodness, forbearance, and longsuffering, not knowing that the goodness of God leads you to repentance?"* God's kindness is responsible for being in the family of God. Titus 3:2 says, *"To speak evil of no man, to be no brawlers, but gentle, shewing all meekness unto all men. For we ourselves were sometimes foolish, disobedient, deceived, serving divers lusts and pleasures, living in malice and envy, hateful, and hating one another. But after that the kindness and love of God our Saviour toward man appeared."*

Do you want to know what that kindness looks like? Watch the kindness of God. While we were not in position to give God anything, He still extended His love, goodness, mercy and grace to us. We are recipients of the kindness of God. And when much is given, much is expected. Sometimes, if we cannot do a big thing, we do not want to do anything. But, the small things can go a long way. Do you have a pleasant tone in your voice? Do you lash out or rip another person with harsh, critical language? Are you sarcastic with your family or friends? When is the last time you gave a card to someone to share how much they mean to you? I am not talking about their birthday or anniversary. When was the last time you expressed love and kindness to your spouse? Your parents? When is the last time you did a random act of kindness? Sent an email just to express appreciation? That is kindness. Can you smile or hold the door for someone? These are small things.

When someone is not kind to you or dogging you out, I know it is not easy to be kind. The great, Black, mystic theologian Howard Thurman was born and grew up in Daytona Beach, Florida. He once talked about a woman who lived next to them when he was growing up. She hated Black people, especially the Thurman family. She hated them so much that she would shovel the manure from her chicken coop into the Thurman's yard every day. Well, you know God don't like ugly! One day, this woman was stricken with a stroke. When she came home from the hospital, she was no longer able to do for herself. One day, Mrs. Thurman went to see her, much to the childish anger and chagrin of Howard Thurman. And when she went to visit her, she took her some freshly cut flowers. Howard Thurman could not understand why his mother would go over to see her. The lady was also surprised Mrs. Thurman came to see her. And when she came in, the woman's eyes lit up. She said, *"I hated you all these years, but you came to visit me on my sick bed. And you brought me some beautiful flowers. Where did these gorgeous flowers come from?"* Mrs. Thurman said, *"You know that manure you were flinging over into my yard every day? I turned that manure into fertilizer. And these flowers came out of that fertilizer. And these are the flowers I brought to you."*

If you are a child of God, if God is your Creator, if Jesus is your Savior, if the Holy Ghost is your helper, there are some people who will throw manure on you. There are some people who will dog you out. There are some people who will do you wrong. But, God will give you the power and ability to make some fertilizer out of that and to give them flowers out of how they have been dogging you. Jesus, one Friday night on Calvary, got some manure on Him. But, He died on the cross, the cross where I first saw the light and the burdens of my heart rolled away. On a hill far away stood an old rugged cross, the emblem of suffering and shame. But one Sunday morning, He changed that manure into fertilizer, and He rose from the dead with all power in His hands! And now, because He lives, I can face tomorrow. Because He lives, all fear is gone. Because I know He holds the future, and life is worth the living just because He lives. God will help you turn manure into fertilizer. Keep on loving. Keep on serving. Keep on being kind. God is able to help you overcome. God will give you victory. Greater is He that is in you, than he that is in the world.

Let us pray: Father, we thank you. We honor you, and we bless your name. Thank you for your power that gives us the ability to love, be kind and be patient. Help us, LORD, to transform the meanness that others show us into goodness and value. Looking at Jesus as our example who turned a dark Friday into a bright resurrection on Sunday morning. Thank you for this now, in Jesus' name. Hallelujah and amen.

Love Unlimited

Chapter 3

LOVE DOES NOT ENVY
1 Corinthians 13:4b NKJV

"Love does not envy..."

Love has many facets. It is like a kaleidoscope with different images and parts to it. When the Apostle Paul wrote about love in 1 Corinthians 13, he gave two positive descriptions of love. He said love is patient and kind. Then, he shifted to show the negative side. In other words, sometimes you have to help people understand what something is by showing them what it is not. He gave 13 examples of what love is not, and at the top of the list was envy. He said love is not envious. The Greek word envy means to boil. It is like the idea of leaving a pot on the stove and forgetting about it. You return to the pot, only to find it has boiled over. That is what envy does when it goes unchecked. In your heart, it boils over. The weed of envy can choke the flower in your heart if you do not pull it out. Envy has disrupted families, fractured friendships, messed up marriages, ruptured relationships, and divided churches. It is, perhaps, the most dangerous vice that can happen to a family or a church, with the exception of its first cousin – pride.

Often times, we use envy and jealousy interchangeably, but there is a slight difference between the two. Envy stands at the bottom of the pile and is mad at who is at the top. Jealousy is at the top of the pile and afraid someone is going to take its place. Envy has its hands empty and is upset because of someone else's possessions. Jealousy has its hands full and afraid someone is going to take it. Envy is upset at what someone else possesses, is doing, or has. Jealousy legitimately has something, but is afraid someone is going to take it.

The Bible talks about God being a jealous God for Israel. A lot of times, jealousy comes out of someone who is insecure. But, God is not insecure. God is protective, and out of a protective love, it says He is jealous. Jealousy is interesting because you may have a spouse who you claim as yours. Your husband. Your wife. You belong to one another and have the papers to prove it. So, it is understandable to be jealous if someone tries to make a move on what is yours. It is not right, but it is understandable. But, envy is more insidious. Envy says, *"I want what you have. I am not content with what I have or what I am doing, or who I am, so I want what you have."*

The Circles of Envy

Envy flows in circles. If you study the Bible, you will notice an interesting concept of many circles where envy shows up. One way it shows up is in possessions. In Genesis 26:14, Isaac had great possessions, and it says the Philistines were envious of him because of what he had. Envy does not say, *"Ah that's a nice sweater. I'd like a sweater like that."* No, envy says, *"I want THAT sweater."* Envy does not see someone driving a fancy car and says, *"Oh, what a nice car. I'd like a car like that."* No, envy says, *"I want THAT car."*

Not only does it show up in the circle of possessions, it also shows up in the circle of power. In the Old Testament, Aaron, Miriam and the sons of Kora, according to Psalm 106:16, were jealous of Moses. They were envious of his leadership because of his power, and they wanted the power he possessed. People can be cut throat, have sharp elbows, or use their power to tear someone else down to get a position. That is how it works in the world. That is how it works on your job. That is how it works in the world of business. Unfortunately, Paul was writing not to a business or workplace, but to the church. Oftentimes, we bring that crappy mentality into the church, but it has no room in the house of God.

There is also a circle of performance. When David brought down Goliath, 1 Samuel 18:7 says, *"The women sang as they danced, and said: Saul had slain his thousands, And David his ten thousands."* When Saul heard that, he was envious and began a campaign to kill David. He believed David was trying to get his position. David was actually Saul's mentee. If Saul had confidence and was not insecure when he heard that, he would have taken it as a compliment, knowing that he taught this young man so well that he was able to slay his 10 thousands. But Saul was envious and insecure, so he did not hear it that way. We sometimes see a circle of performance in the church. That is when you see people doing something, and you want to do what they are doing instead of walking in your own gift, ability and calling. You have to understand that God has given every one of us gifts, and we need one another. In the chapter before this one, Paul talked about how the church is a body and how we need each other. If you are the ear and I am the eye, I cannot put you down because I need you to hear and you need me to see. If you are the leg and I am the foot, I cannot say you are not valuable because I need you to get around and you need me to stand. We are a body of Christ, and we need one another. If someone is doing something, God also has a calling for you to do something in the church, too.

Envy also travels in the circle of professionalism. In Philippians 1:15, there were preachers who were envious of Paul's ministry. These were fellow preachers. They were preaching the gospel, not out of a sincere love for God, but out of envy for the Apostle Paul. Paul rejoiced and said, whether they are doing it out of sincerity or not, at least the gospel is preached. Envy could even show up in *your* profession or career.

But worst of all, envy can show up in families. Cain killed Abel. Isaac mocked Ishmael. Jacob tricked his brother out of his birthright. Even Jesus was rejected by his own family. One of the best examples of this is in Genesis 37. Joseph, who was Jacob's favorite son, received a coat of many colors from his father. His brothers became envious. As a side note, let me say this to the ladies. If you have a man who had children prior to your relationship with him, and now he has children with you, let him love both sets of children because you have no idea how much bitterness and anger can show up in the heart of a child when he knows his father has given love to other children and did not do it for them.

The Course of Envy

What happens when envy travels and is unchecked? It destroys the object of envy. There ought to be something in you that stands up for truth and does not want to pull somebody down. But, when you are envious, you do not care, as long as that person is destroyed. There ought to be something inside of you that even if you hear a lie, you will say, *"No, that is not right,"* even if you do not like the person. Even if that is your enemy. Right is right and wrong is wrong. You should not want to see a person destroyed over an untruth. Envy destroys its object; the object of envy.

Whoever you are transferring envy to, you would do anything to destroy that person. The Bible tells us to rejoice with those who rejoice and weep with those who weep, but envy rejoices with those who weep and weeps when people rejoice. It destroys its object.

Worse than even that, envy destroys its subject. It destroys not only the one who you are envious of, but also the person who is envious. Envy is like acid in a container that destroys the container. That is what envy does to the one who is envious. It destroys its own. In his writings, Italian writer/philosopher Dante depicted envious people in hell with their eyelids shut. It dramatizes the notion that envious people cannot see beyond themselves. So, it is with envy that envy destroys the person who is envious. While you are angry, envious, and jealous of someone else, you do not realize it is destroying you. When you dig one ditch, you better dig two because, as the saints of old would say, *"The trap you set for somebody else may just be for you, and you can't keep somebody down in the ditch without staying there yourself."* Daniel's friends, who threw him in the lion's den, got crushed by the lions. Joseph was much better off than his brothers who were in famine – even though they threw him into the pit. David was in the wilderness with confidence in God, but Saul, who was envious, could not even sleep because he was full of envy. I am telling you, envy destroys its subject.

The Cure for Envy

You may be asking yourself, *"How do I overcome and get beyond envy? I'm wrestling with this, and I really want to uproot this weed that's in my heart choking out love."* Well, the first step is to renounce envy and jealousy and confess it as sin. 1 Peter 2:1 says,

"Therefore, laying aside all malice, all deceit, hypocrisy, envy, and all evil speaking." Malice means to tear someone down. Deceit means to use untruths to do it. Hypocrisy means to be disingenuous. And, it is all rooted in envy. Just like people, words are known by the company they keep. The word envy is surrounded by malice – *"I have to tear you down."* Deceit – *"I have to use lies to tear you down."* Hypocrisy – *"I have to act like something I'm not."* Evil speaking – *"I have to speak evil of you."* It is all rooted in envy. It is sin. Matthew 27:18 says, *"For he knew that they handed Him over because of envy."* This Scripture refers to Pontius Pilate. The enemies of Jesus put Him on the cross because of envy. Envy is sin, so confess it as sin. Simply say, *"LORD, I'm sorry I missed the mark. I've been envious."*

The second step is to remember your rival in prayer. Start praying for your rival; the one you are envious over; the one you are upset with. Start praying for them every day this week in your prayer time. Spend five minutes praying for them. It could be your coworker or a family member. Whoever it is, pray for them. Jesus instructed us to love our enemies and pray for those who spitefully use us. It is hard to hate somebody you are praying for. If you really want to know liberation and freedom, pray for your rival. Pray for your enemy.

The third step is to reaffirm God's goodness to you and learn to be content with what you have. Oftentimes, we are envious of somebody else because we do not understand that God has already blessed us. Paul said in Philippians 4:11-12, *"Not that I speak in regard of need, for I have learned in whatever state I am, to be content: I know how to be abased, and I know how to abound. Everywhere and in all things I have learned both to be full and to be hungry, both to abound and to suffer need."* I've learned how to be content. I may not be content *with* it, but I am content *in* it. If I have to eat spaghetti three days in a row instead of filet mignon, I am still content because I have something to eat. I learned how to say thank you for what I have. I may not be able to shop at the stores I want, but thank God for JC with a Penny! Thank God for Walmart. Thank God for clothes on my back. I am thankful for what I have. No, that is not my dream car, but I have something that can take me from point A to point B.

The final step to overcome envy is to rekindle God's love in your heart through prayer and the word. You need to do this because it is hard for love to grow if the weed of envy is in the garden of your heart. It will choke it. I pray you begin to pluck that out of your heart today. God wants you to be free instead of all bound up.

Let us pray: Father God, we thank you and honor you for who you are. You are such an awesome God and deliverer. God, we thank you for your mercy and grace. We thank you for your power and strength. Now God, I am asking that you would now, in the name of Jesus, help us to remove envy and jealousy out of our hearts and replace it with your love. Replace it with your grace. Not just charisma, but compassion. LORD, forgive us for walking in envy. LORD, we confess today that we have not been the children you want us to be. We renounce it today. LORD, we thank you for what we have. We are content because we have a reason to say thank you for whatever we have, even with issues and problems. You have been so good to us, so in the midst of it today, we say thank you. Through heartache, pains and problems, we say thank you. LORD, we just bless your name for your goodness and mercy. God, help us to rekindle that in our hearts. Give us the fire of love for one another. In Jesus' name we say hallelujah and amen.

Love Unlimited

Love is Not Full of Pride
1 Corinthians 13:4b NKJV

"...[Love] is not puffed up."

A subway car in our nation's capital had an advertisement that read, *"The best bank in the best city for the best person - you."* Other than being advertisement hype, there was a time when those words would have been offensive. But, at a time where CEOs are bigger than companies, presidents are larger than institutions, players are bigger than teams, orchestra musicians are larger than orchestras, and even preachers are bigger than churches, that type of advertisement is acceptable. This nation has become trumped because of pride. You can put your name on a hotel, a casino, and even an airplane. It is the horrible sin of pride.

Some 1,500 years ago when the church decided to list the seven sins, there was envy, gluttony, murder, etc., and at the top of the list was pride. Now at the very front porch of this message, I want to be clear about what pride is *not*. If you have confidence or a sense of accomplishment, that is not pride. In fact, the African Church Father Augustine called that modest pride, and he said you need that. If you prepare a meal for someone, and they enjoy that meal, you may have a sense of satisfaction. That is fine. That is not pride. Our students have invested their time and commitment in their education, and they now have diplomas, certificates and degrees. You feel a sense of accomplishment for their hard work. That is not pride. That is just a sense of confidence and accomplishment. If you have successfully built a home with your bare hands, that is not pride. That is a sense of accomplishment. But when the Bible speaks of pride, it means having an attitude that puts you in a space that is reserved only for God. It is the idea that you can screw in a light bulb without turning your wrist because the world revolves around you.

When the Apostle Paul used the phrase *puffed up,* he was talking to the church of Corinth, and if we were at that church, we would find some very arrogant, pompous, insular, self-serving, and self-absorbed church people. Paul was trying to get them to understand what love was. He had already shared with them that love is patient and kind, but he shifted and told them love does not envy, and it is not prideful. He started the phrase about being puffed up in 1 Corinthians 5 when he was writing to them because there was sin in the church. There was a man who was sleeping with his father's wife, and Paul said he was puffed up about it. The sin itself was bad enough, but it was his cavalier, casual attitude that made it worse. He was prideful and puffed up about it. Then in 1 Corinthians 8, he spoke on an argument about food being eaten that was offered to idols. The people were very knowledgeable and gifted, but they were puffed up. Paul shared how knowledge puffs up, but love builds up.

Pride Ignores God's Sovereignty

Paul talked about pride and tried to show them the importance of the church having love. One of the things that keeps the flower of love from growing in the garden of the church is the weed of pride. What is it about pride that hurts love? Well, for one thing, it ignores the sovereignty of God. You can become so arrogant after your success that you feel you do not need anything, not even God. Who is it that made you who you are? I Corinthians 4:7

says, *"For who makes you differ from another? And what do you have that you did not receive?"* James said it like this, *"Every good and perfect gift comes from God."* John said, *"There is nothing that you received that did not come from the father."* Paul was trying to convey this simple message. You may be successful and accomplished, but you did not do it on your own. You need to understand and recognize that whatever things you have amassed and accomplished, it is nothing but the grace and goodness of God. That is why you cannot laugh at other people or get haughty and uppity. It is but by the grace of God. If God removed His hand from you, you would not be where you are, who you are, or what you are.

Some of you get successful and no longer have time for the church, but if it was not for the church, if it was not for those women praying for you, if it was not for an old deacon having you on his mind, if it was not for a preacher loving you, if it was not for a Sunday school teacher that told you about Jesus and told Jesus about you, you would not be where you are. Do not forget where you came from!

Pride Invites God's Judgment

Not only does pride ignore the sovereignty of God, it also invites the judgment of God. You may be thinking, *"I'm not the one who is prideful. Actually, I'm being abused and misused by someone who is prideful."* It could be a boss, a prideful supervisor, or a prideful professor or teacher. My message to you is…God is in control. Just give Him time because God confronts pride. In Isaiah 14:12, Satan was the top angel in heaven. He was the principal angel of worship. But the problem was, he forgot who he was worshipping and wanted to be worshipped. He got high in that space that was reserved only for God. The prophecy in Isaiah 14:12 was a backward view of Satan. He said, *"How art thou fallen from heaven, O Lucifer, son of the morning! how art thou cut down to the ground, which didst weaken the nations! For thou hast said in thine heart, I will ascend into heaven, I will exalt my throne above the stars of God: I will sit also upon the mount of the congregation, in the sides of the north: I will ascend above the heights of the clouds; I will be like the most High. Yet thou shalt be brought down to hell, to the sides of the pit. They that see thee shall narrowly look upon thee, and consider thee, saying, 'Is this the man that made the earth to tremble, that did shake kingdoms'."* In other words, a time will come where we will look at Satan and say, *"You're the one that's been causing all this havoc? You're the one who got so high in your mind that God had to bring you down?"*

A few years ago, there was a Russian SU 24 jet that was in Turkish airspace; an area where it did not belong. For 10 minutes they gave five warnings telling it to leave, but it would not leave. After 10 minutes, two S16 bombers shot the jet down because it was in an airspace that it did not belong. Whenever you get so prideful, arrogant and insular in your mind, and think you are the greatest, nobody can bother you, and you do not need anyone including God, you are in a space where you do not belong. Thank God He is merciful! He will send you warnings, but if you miss out on the warnings, God will bring you down.

Pride invites God's judgment. Not only did it happen to Satan, but it happened to a king called Nebuchadnezzar in Daniel 4. God actually used Nebuchadnezzar to discipline Israel. Nebuchadnezzar was king of Babylon, and Babylon overtook Judah. They were oppressed in exile for some 70 years. King

Love Unlimited

Nebuchadnezzar had a dream one day, and he could not find anyone to interpret it. Then, he called the Prophet Daniel and told him about his dream. His dream was about a tree with branches that went all around the world. Even birds began to nest in it. Suddenly, something came out of heaven and cut the tree down. Only the stump remained. Daniel revealed to King Nebuchadnezzar that the dream was not about his enemies, but about him. He would be cut down for seven years until he recognized that God was God. Nebuchadnezzar did not get the warning. Daniel 4:28-30 says, *"All this came upon King Nebuchadnezzar. At the end of twelve months he walked in the palace of the kingdom of Babylon. The king spake, and said, Is not this great Babylon, that I have built for the house of the kingdom by the might of my power, and for the honour of my Majesty?"* Watch *i* and *my*. Whenever your world revolves around *i* and *my*, you are in trouble. That is called pride. Do you recognize that pride is a sin that has *i* in the middle? Whenever *i* is in the middle, you will get in trouble. Sin: s-i-n. Lie: l-i-e. Whenever *i* is in the middle, it is a slippery slope.

"While the word was in the king's mouth, there fell a voice from heaven, saying, O king Nebuchadnezzar, to thee it is spoken; The kingdom is departed from thee. And they shall drive thee from men." It had gotten so bad for the king, he literally became like an animal. His kingdom was like a pasture, and for seven years he groped around like a ruminating animal until he recognized that God was God. It does not matter how successful you are, when you are caught up in pride and God confronts and judges it, you are going down.

A few years ago, I was in Paris, France and stood at Napoleon's tomb. Napoleon was a great warrior. It is interesting because the tomb is really five coffins in one. It is one coffin of lead, another coffin of green granite, one of black marble, and one of green marble. It is a thing inside a thing. I do not know why they put him in five coffins. Maybe they wanted to ensure he did not get out! But Napoleon was such a mass ruler and brilliant military strategist, there are some areas of our justice system and education system that were crafted and taken from Napoleon. That is how awesome he was. But he got so prideful, he wanted to take over Russia. He did it in the winter time which was the worst time to try to attack them because Russia has horrible winters. It got so bad that the mayor of Moscow burned the city so that Napoleon could not take it over. His own people advised him to wait until the spring. But, when you are caught up in pride, you do not even listen to common sense. He charged 500,000 soldiers to go toward Russia, and they died in Russia's winter. Then, Napoleon was banished to an island about 10,000 miles off of the coast of North Africa. He died alone because no matter how high you get, when God gets ready to bring you down, you are going down.

Pride Can be Interrupted by God's Recognition

If you will recognize who God is, it can save you from pride. Let me give you seven quick tips to help you overcome the spirit of pride.

One - See the glory of God. When you see God's glory, it gives you a sense of awe in how great God is and how small you are. It helps you understand how significant God is and how insignificant you are. Then you begin to understand that everything you have is because of God. That is what Isaiah saw in Isaiah 6. It says, *"In the year that King Uzziah died I saw the Lord* *sitting on a throne, high and lifted up, and the train of His robe filled the temple. Above it stood the seraphim; each one had six wings: with two he covered his face, with two he covered his feet, with two he flew. And one cried to another and said: holy, holy, holy is the LORD of hosts; the whole earth is full of His glory!"* And what did Isaiah say? He did not say how wonderful he was. He said, *"Woe is me, for I am undone! Because I am a man of unclean lips; And I dwell in the midst of a people of unclean lips; For my eyes have seen the King, The LORD of hosts."* When you really get close to God, you will not see how holy *you* are. No, you will see how hellish and messed up you are. When you really get close and intimate with God, you do not say *"I'm all that!"* You should say, *"Woe is me! God help me because I can't make without you."*

Two - Appreciate correction from people who care about you. There are some people who may not tell you what you want to hear, but they tell you what you need to hear. It is not because they are being critical, but because they love you enough to tell you the truth.

Three - Settle all differences as soon as possible. In Romans 12:18, Paul says, *"If it is possible, as much as depends on you, live peaceably with all men."* This means you take the initiative to correct the situation. I know some people do not want to be reconciled. You cannot do anything about that, but at least you would have extended your hand for there to be reconciliation.

Four - Stop expecting people to be perfect when you are not. Do not compare yourself to other people. You are on your journey. They are on their journey. Whenever you compare yourself to somebody, you can always find somebody worse than you, but they are not the standard of measurement. See, when you put yourself up against Damone Paul Johnson, you may be a spiritual giant compared to me, but I am not the standard of measurement. Jesus is the standard of measurement. When you put yourself up against God, you are going to see just how tiny and small you really are.

Five - Do not brag on yourself. Proverbs 27:2 says, *"Let another man praise you, and not your own mouth."* Watch that bragging on yourself. Bragging and being prideful is an interesting disease because pride makes everybody sick around it except the person who has it.

Six - Have someone who you can be accountable to; someone who can keep you grounded. When you are not grounded, you are like a balloon full of helium. The balloon will rise up unless someone is holding it down. Like the balloon, you need someone who can hold you and keep you grounded because if not, you can rise up. You need somebody who can bring you back down. When you accomplish some goals and reach a level of success, you may start to rise back up. You may get a college degree and begin to rise on up. You may get the car or house you want, but you need somebody who sees you in a space you do not belong in and help bring you back down. When you do not have people in your life who can bring you back down, you will rise up to a space where you do not belong. You do not want to do that.

Seven – Humble yourself. Now here is what messed me up. Nowhere in the Bible does it say to pray for humility. You do not ever want to pray for humility. Do not pray for God to make you humble. The Bible says in 1 Peter 5 to humble yourself under the mighty hand of God. Humble yourself because you do not want God to have to humble you. We just read what happened to

Love Unlimited

Satan and Nebuchadnezzar. The Bible says humble yourself so God does not have to. There is a difference between humility and humiliation. Humility is when you humble yourself. Humiliation is when somebody else humbles you. You have never heard anyone say, *"I humiliated myself."* You may have embarrassed yourself - stumbled and fell, had a slip of the tongue - but you cannot humiliate yourself. Somebody else has to humiliate you. That is why you should humble yourself. God resists the proud, and He gives grace to the humble. The word *resist* literally means God gets an army around Him and He mounts a plan to bring the prideful person down. When you carry the ball of pride, God becomes a linebacker whose job is to tackle the one with pride and bring him down. You do not want God to be a linebacker, tackling and bringing you down, so humble yourself.

If you are wondering what happened to King Nebuchadnezzar, let me finish telling you that story. After seven years, he looked up and he repented and said, God is God. And, guess what? God restored Him! Now, I hope it does not take you seven years to recognize that God is God. You can recognize it today. You can be like that prodigal son in Luke 15 who took his inheritance, went out, and squandered everything he had. But the Bible says he came to himself while in a pig pen, and he went back another way. If you have been operating in the spirit of pride, today you can recognize that God is God. The good news is if you will return back to Him, God will receive you, forgive you, love you, and restore you because He is such a loving, gracious and good God!

Let us pray: Heavenly Father, we thank you for your generous portion of grace and mercy. We know it is you and you alone who have created us and given us all our abilities. We recognize you in all our accomplishments. Father God, we rebuke the spirit of pride. Help us to always recognize your sovereignty in our lives. In Jesus' name we pray, Amen.

Chapter 5

LOVE IS NOT RUDE
1 Corinthians 13:5a NKJV

"...[Love] does not behave rudely..."

As believers, it is important for us to understand God expects us to exhibit a God-kind of love. It is one that seeks only the best for someone. The Greeks have many words for love. One of them is eros, which is a romantic or lustful type of love. So, when someone says, *"I love you,"* sometimes they mean *I lust you*. There is another type of love called philia, which means a friendly type of love. But, the God kind of love is a love that wants the best, and it is called agape love. It is not like philia, the love for a friend. The city of Philadelphia is named after philia love. It is a friend love. The type of love the Apostle Paul talked about in 1 Corinthians 13 is a God-type of agape love that is selfless.

Apparently, the believers in Corinth were not acting loving in the body of Christ, so Paul shared with them what love is. He said love is kind, love is patient, love gives to someone who does not deserve it and holds back the wrath that one does deserve. Again, Paul said love is not envious, love is not prideful, and love is not rude. Rude means to be out of shape or not behave itself seemly. Have you ever seen people who always do something at the wrong time? They ought to be encouraging but they are discouraging. They should be positive, but they are negative. You can always rely on them for something negative, nasty and bad to come out their mouth. That is not love. That is why Paul posits the point to understand what love is not.

I am thankful the word of God gives us principles, practices, performances and pictures to make a point. In 1 Samuel 25 there is a picture of what it is to be courteous, and there is a picture of what it is to be rude. Come with me to Carmel. There was a couple there by the name of Nabal and Abigail. Nabal had sheep and goats. He was a very successful businessman. Abigail, his wife, was a sensitive person. In this couple, one was rude and one was courteous. One showed love and one did not.

One of Nabal's issues was the meaning of his name. It means fool. He lived up to his name, too. He walked like a fool, talked like a fool, and acted like a fool. I know the Bible says not to call anybody a fool, but I am not calling him a fool. I am just calling him what his name in verse 25 literally means. Before I unpack this, just let me say something to the single people who are reading this. Be careful who you marry because if he is not right while you are single, he will not get right just because you marry him. You are fooling yourself if you think, *"Well, as long as he is with me, he'll be right!"* No, that is the wrong perspective. If he is not right in God and if God does not change him, he will not be right after the wedding.

Love Unlimited

David was on his way to becoming the King. God fired King Saul, but David was not King yet. While David was on his way to becoming king, he was actually running from Saul before he reached an area called Carmel. Nabal lived in Maon, but Carmel was where his sheep and goats were. David, along with his 600 men, were protecting that area. They had been like a wall of defense and protection. After a while, it was a time of celebration, so David sent some of his servants to Nabal, the business owner, to ask for a portion of what he had because David and his men had been protecting his land and livestock. They did not charge anything or take anything. They also ensured no one else took anything. Even Nabal's servants could verify that. It was a time of celebration, partying and enjoyment, and they just wanted a portion for their celebration. Nabal said, *"I'm not giving you anything."*

This story amazes me because this was Nabal who had something but would not give a portion to the king. But, do not get mad at Nabal because there are some of us who have some things but refuse to give anything to the King of Kings. Please understand that courtesy and generosity go together. If you see someone who is not courteous, you also see someone who is selfish. If you see someone who is rude, that person is selfish, self-serving and self-absorbed. This neighbor was selfish, and he was not generous. He had something, but would not give a little bit to the king. Now, if David wanted to, he could have taken everything he was protecting. Nabal, who did not understand that King David was protecting his sheep, refused to give anything to the king, even though he had something to give. Some of us who have nothing have found a way to give something. We can find a good example of this in Mark chapter 12. There was a widow who had two mites, and she gave these two mites. Mites are small. It is where we get the word *minute* from. When Jesus looked at the offering, he noticed there were some wealthy givers who gave a lot. He told His disciples that the woman who gave two mites actually gave more than those who gave the big amount. When they questioned why, He explained it was because she gave everything that she had.

In 2 Corinthians chapter 8, the Apostle Paul talks about the churches in Macedonia and how they gave beyond their ability, even though they were poor churches. How do you give beyond your ability? If you have a desire to give, God will make a way for you to give. It amazes me how God has provided so much for so many of us, and yet we give nothing back to Him. We do not do it in other areas of our lives. We will find a way to give. Many of you cannot afford that car you are driving, but you are driving it. Many of you cannot afford that house, but you are living in it. Some of you have maxed your credit cards out just to wear the clothes you are wearing. You give beyond your ability. If you can do that for a car, a house, and for clothes, why can't you do that for the King of Kings?

David's men said to Nabal, *"Peace and prosperity be unto you and to your family."* He went and offered him peace, even though Nabal was being stingy. When God gives you peace personally, when God gives you peace to your family, and when God gives you peace ultimately, you ought to have a desire to give Him back a portion of what He has given to you. He said peace *and* prosperity because it is possible to have prosperity but not have peace. Some people live in a big house but hate to go home. You have prosperity but no peace. You have a beautiful car, but no peace of mind when you are driving down the street. You have prosperity but no peace. You have a king-sized bed but you toss and turn all night, getting no sleep because you are worried and concerned about something. That is prosperity without peace.

But, God is able to give you prosperity *and* peace. I have discovered that my faith level is such that no matter when I give to God, I expect Him to provide for me. When I give to the LORD, I expect Him to preserve, protect and provide for me. It does not matter if there is inflation. It does not matter what the economy does. I depend on Jehovah Jireh, not job jireh! I have been walking with God long enough to know He is able to provide every one of my needs. He that keeps Israel neither slumbers nor does He sleep.

In spite of the prosperity and peace God has provided, some of you will not give to God. One sickness can wipe all your savings out. Unemployment for just six weeks can mess you up financially, and yet, we know there is a God who is able to preserve you in prosperity or poverty. God will protect you. God will preserve you. God will watch over you. Now, you may have to go through something, but God is able to preserve and protect you. There are people who have gone through less than you, and they put a bullet to their head or slit their wrist. They have jumped off bridges, but the reason why you have not lost your mind is because of the peace of God that has helped and sustained you. What I have been going through personally, I could have lost my mind months ago, but I am here because the peace of God held me even in the dark times.

I am trying to figure out why would this one man who had all this stuff not give anything to the king. One reason was ignorance. In fact, he asked who David was. *Who is Jesse's son in the first place?* Interestingly, Nabal acted like he did not know who David was. His wife knew who he was. His servants knew who he was. All of Israel knew who he was. This was David, the giant slayer who slew Goliath. This was David, the one who brought down the Philistines. This was David who the women were singing about, *"Saul has slayed his thousands, but David his tens of thousands."* How did Nabel not know? Some of you do not give because *you* do not understand who it is that has been helping you. You do not know it was Jesus who saved your soul. Washed your sins away. Made you whole. Provided for you. Kept you.

The average church has 20 percent of its members who give 80 percent of the money. It does not matter if it is a Black, white, Hispanic or other church. It does not matter if it is Baptist, Methodist or COGIC.

Love Unlimited

At Metropolitan Church, our numbers are slightly higher. About 30 percent of those who attend or watch give just about all of the money. There is about another 20 percent who give about $5 or $10 every now and then. That means there is 50 percent who do not give anything. Out of all the attendees and those watching online, half of the people are not giving anything. They get the same message, same music, same ministry, and the same minister that the rest are getting, but do not give. I am trying to figure out why people will not provide, even when God has blessed and helped them? For Nabal, it was ignorance. But it was not just ignorance, it was also arrogance. He said, *"I'm not going to give my money or my meat to you."* I told you he was a fool. He sounds like another fool in Luke 12, the one who had all these barns that were filled. That fool said, *"I'm going to tear down these barns and build bigger ones. I'm going to eat, drink, and be merry."* God said he was a fool because that night, his soul would be required of him. What would it profit a man to gain the whole world and lose his soul? Some of us do not understand that we have what we have because of God.

Some years ago, at the Indianapolis Zoo, there was a radiated tortoise that was on loan from a country in Africa. It was on exhibit for a few months. But one day, the director of the exhibit came in and noticed the radiated tortoise was gone. They found it seven days later on 64th and Meridian on a running trail called Holiday Park. Indianapolis is the 12th largest city in America. Indianapolis Zoo is downtown. Sixty-Fourth and Meridian is about 10 miles away. The director of the exhibit said there was no way the tortoise could have gotten out of the gated enclosure and navigated his way to 64th and Meridian, one of the busiest streets in the city, and landed at that trail. He said somebody had to have lifted him up and then carried him to where he was found. Some of you were in bondage, and there was no way you got out of that bondage unless God lifted you up. No wonder we sing, *"I'm so glad Jesus lifted me!"* There is no way you would have gotten where you are unless somebody had brought you there. If you would be honest with yourself, you would understand that you are like a radiated tortoise - you are somebody who God has lifted up. Somebody who God has brought a mighty long way. There is somebody who is smarter than you, looks better than you, who is more intelligent than you, but do not have what you have. It was no one but Jesus who made a way. You have what you have because of the grace and favor of God.

Let us pray: LORD, we honor and thank you today. Thank you for bringing us and lifting us up. Thank you for guiding us and bringing us on the right path. Now God, help us not to be stingy and rude. Help us to be loving to the King and to the King's people; to the Father and to His children. We pray this in Jesus' name. Hallelujah and amen.

Chapter 6

Love Is Courteous
1 Corinthians 13:5a KJV

"[Love] doth not behave itself unseemly..."

Have you ever walked into a church you thought would be welcoming and hospitable, but instead, people were mean, arrogant and rude? Well, if you had gone on Sunday morning to the church of Corinth, that is what you would have found. The ushers were rude. The people were mean. And, if you needed a place to sit, people would not get out the way to make room for you to sit.

As I mentioned previously, there was a whole cadre of things going on at the church of Corinth when Paul wrote 1 Corinthians 13 – fractures in the fellowship, suing saints, assorted sexual sins – and at the heart of it was a lack of love. He knew that if they got love straight, a lot of the other things would take care of themselves. In verse 5, it says, "It [love] does not behave itself unseemly." In other words, love is not rude, it's courteous.

I love how the Bible gives us principles to practice and pictures to see the principle. In the previous chapter, we looked at a businessman named Nabal as an illustration of what rudeness looks like. The opposite of rudeness is to be courteous; extending kindness; hospitable. In that story,

Nabal was foolish in how he dealt with his servants, his material possessions, and his actions. To recap, David and his men were guarding Nabal's sheep and goats because they settled in Carmel for a little while. When they asked Nabal for a portion of what he had because they watched over his livestock, Nabal said no. I am not giving you anything.

God can provide so much to us, and we can be so stingy with Him. Nabal had something, but did not want to give anything. Some people have nothing, but end up giving *something* to the LORD. An example is the churches in Macedonia that Paul writes about in 2 Corinthians chapters 8 and 9. He said those churches had nothing to give, but had the desire to give. When they had the desire to give, God provided the means for them to give. If you really have a heart to give with little resources, God will make a way for you to give, *if* you have a desire.

Whether you have prosperity or poverty, God can give you some peace. Some of you may be thinking you do not have much. You may be struggling right now. But understand that God can still give you peace, even with poverty. In the midst of everything you may be going through, I know some of you reading this book may be able to testify that God has kept you, He has held you, and He has given you peace that surpasses all understanding.

On September 11, 2001, when the planes hit the Twin Towers in New York City, 1.2 billion tons of steel were burned. A ton is 2,000 pounds. But we are talking about 1.2 billion tons that went down. Nothing was recognizable. Not a chair. Not an office. Not a person. But then the cleanup crew found two beams as they were cleaning up the area. One was horizontal and one was vertical. In the midst of all that wreckage, they came across... *a cross*. Even in the midst of chaos and calamity, Christ shows up with His cross. Even in midst of the most dangerous time of ruin and destruction, He is still with you. Some of you have been in chaos, calamity and destruction, but Christ has shown up. God is with you. He will not leave you or forsake you. No matter what you are going through, and no matter what you have to face in the midst of your chaos, God will show up with His cross!

Now let us take a look at Nabal's wife, Abigail. When Nabal told David he would give him nothing, David got upset. David told his men to strap up. They were on their way to go get Nabal and destroy everything he had, including all of his servants. One of Nabal's servants overheard this and reported it to Abigail. So, Abigail began to extend courtesy. She loaded up some gifts and told her servant to take them to David. She wanted the servant to meet David and his men en route before they got there because destruction was coming to their house. Abigail did not allow Nabal's rudeness to make her rude.

You do not have to be rude because somebody else is. You do not have to be mean and nasty to somebody because your friends are. You do not have to be mean because your co-workers are.

Abigail was in a male-dominated society. She was devalued and looked at as property. Even though she was married to a fool, she operated in wisdom. She moved with immediacy. Abigail was in a hurry to get the gifts to David because she understood destruction was coming to her house. For some people, you are putting something off right now. What are you putting off? What are you waiting for? It could be the issue of your faith when you know you should get right with God. You know you need to be on prayer calls and weekly Bible studies, but you keep putting it off. You can even watch Bible study online from anywhere in the world without even going to church, so there is no excuse. You can log into Facebook or YouTube. You know you should be going to Sunday School, but you keep saying, *"I'll go next time. I'll go next month. I'll go next year."* You keep putting off getting right with God. If it is not in the area of your faith, maybe it is the area of your family. Maybe you need to start spending more time with your children or taking your marriage seriously. Why do you keep putting it off? Maybe it is not faith or family, but finances. Maybe you really need to start tithing and recognizing that God is the source of everything you have. You need to put Him first; the first tenth belongs to him. Maybe you need to stop buying whatever you want and begging for everything you need! Maybe you need to be a good steward because God has ownership of not only the 10 percent, but everything you have. Everything is under the umbrella of His authority because He provides everything you have. Maybe you need to get serious about saving, investing, and getting rid of credit card debt. You need to get serious about your finances, but some of you keep putting it off. Is the area you are putting off in faith? Family? Finances? It is never too soon to get serious about serious things.

We speak of time as tri-dimensional: past, present and future. I know why they call it the present, because it is just that. It is a present. Every time you wake up in the morning and the sun rises in the east and sets in the west, it is a gift from God; a present. Every time you wake up with blood running warm in your veins, that is something you did not deserve. That is a gift. That is a present. What are you doing with your present? Think about it. When you keep giving someone a gift and they keep throwing it aside, you will eventually say, *"No more presents!"* Every time you wake up in the morning, it is a gift from God, and I wonder what you are doing with your present. Are you wasting your present, or are you using your present? You need to stop saying next time or next week, because no one promised you next week. All you really have is now. If you are going to get your life straight, you need to do it now. If you are going to come to Jesus, you need to do it now. If you are going to get serious about your faith, you need to do it now. If you are going to write that book, you need to write it now. If you are going to finish that class, you need to finish it now. If you are going to finish that project, you need to do it right now!

Abigail got in a hurry. She could not wait. In her intervention, she brought the king gifts because she did not want to be in the presence of the king without a gift. What I love about this is, she did not give to the king because he did not have anything. Verse 13 says 400 men went with David and another 200 stayed with the stuff. That means, the king already had some stuff, even though Abigail gave him more. If you give to the LORD, it does not mean He does not have anything. My Bible says, *"The earth is the LORD's and the fulness thereof; the world, and they that dwell therein!"* The cattle on a thousand hills belong to the LORD. And as the older folks would say, *"The hills belong to Him too!"* He has everything. So, it is not like He does not have stuff.

If Abigail did not want to be in the presence of David without a gift, how can you come into the house of the LORD without a gift? You do not go anywhere else without paying. Do you want to watch your favorite team at a football game? You have to pay to go to their house. Do you want to go to a basketball game? You have to pay to go to their house. Do you want to go to a concert? You pay before you go. Even in the club, you pay the cover charge and have a two drink minimum. And you still go there and pay it. How is it you can pay for the football game, the basketball game, the concert, and the club, but you want to go to the house of God and not give Him anything?

King David said to Abigail, *"It's a good thing you got to me because we were on our way to bring destruction to your house. We were going to kill Nabal and everyone. But because you stepped in, we are not going to kill your husband."* Abigail interceded for Nabal. He did not know it immediately. When she got home, she was going to tell him, but he had thrown a party for himself like he was the king, and he got drunk. This prevented Abigail from telling her husband what she had done. I wonder if our communication and relationships would be better if we stayed sober. Maybe our communication would be better if we sobered up a little bit. She could not tell him. She had to wait until the next day because he was drunk. But she had to intercede for him. Her stepping in is what kept him alive. Some of you have been slipping and sliding, dipping and dodging. You think you are slick, but you are not. Someone has been praying for you. You think you have been getting away with stuff, but you have not. Someone has been praying for you. Either a momma, a daddy, grandparents, a pastor, a brother. Someone has been praying for you. I love this story because Abigail interceded for her husband. And sometimes that is what you have to do for your family. That is what you have to do for your children and grandchildren. You have to intercede and pray even when they do not have enough sense to pray for themselves. Sometimes you have to say, *"LORD, I do not want destruction to come to their house, so I am intervening for them!"*

When we examine this story, we recognize there are consequences for rudeness and courtesy. Scripture tells us the consequence for Nabal's rudeness was sickness and death. He did not handle his material resources right. He did not handle his wife right. He partied hard and was foolish. He was rude and mean. He had a stroke, and 10 days later, he died. Some of you are sick. You are sick of your job. Sick of your house. Sick of your marriage. Sick of this and that. Well, it could be because you are not dealing with God properly when it comes to your resources. When you do not deal with God right with your resources and are rude to the LORD, one of the consequences is it can make you sick.

Now, there are consequences to being courteous as well. When Nabal died, Abigail was back on the market. David sent word to her from one of his servants. He wanted Abigail to be his wife, and she said yes. She went from a ruined and ruptured relationship to a royal relationship. Since she was married to the king who had everything, she had everything. Not only did she have a relationship, but she acquired some resources too. All because she put God first.

You might be thinking your relationships and resources are messed up. Maybe you do not even have a relationship. But ask yourself, how are you treating the King; our LORD? How are you treating your faith? You could be having issues with relationships and resources because it is a consequence for how you are dealing with the King and your material resources; your giving or the lack thereof.

A few years ago, my wife and I went to the Urban League Classic. I grew up in Indianapolis, Indiana, and they had the Circle City Classic. This is where two Historically Black Colleges & Universities play against each other in the Battle of the Bands. The one in New Jersey is called the Urban League Classic, and it is held at the Giants Stadium. We were invited to go. The person who invited us to go told us his company had a suite at the Giants Stadium. He told us where to enter to receive an all-access pass. The all-access pass allowed us to go to the suite area. We met all kinds of big wigs in there; vice presidents and CEOs of companies. We were able to also go down to the field where the action was because we had all access. Security did not bother us. We even got to go behind the scenes where the celebrities were eating and hanging out. Security just let us through. They only looked to make sure we had the all-access pass. And it is all because we were in good relationship with this particular person. Because we were in right relationship, we had access to everything else.

Likewise, when you get it right with the LORD, you get all access. You get access to joy, and peace and faith! When you get it right with God, you get all access. The Bible says all things consist within Him. There are all kinds of blessings, all because you are connected to Him. God will access the windows of heaven to pour you out blessings that you will not have room enough to receive. God will give you access!

Let us pray: Oh, God, we honor you and thank you. We bless you and honor your name today. You are awesome and a great God. LORD, forgive us for being rude and stingy and for being governed by greed and selfishness because you have been so good to us. You have provided for us, preserved us, protected us, and gave us peace and prosperity. How dare we not be fair to you! How dare we be rude to the Father and the Father's children! LORD, forgive us today. Give us a heart of love - your love - to display to you and your children. Thank you for the access we have to the blessings you have for us. We pray this in Jesus' name. Hallelujah and amen.

Chapter 7

LOVE IS NOT SELFISH
1 Corinthians 13:5

"[Love] Does not seek its own."

So many of us desire and are praying for various gifts. Some, the gift to speak. Some, healing. Some, prophesy or preaching. Some, giving. But Paul says the most excellent gift is not the gift of faith, knowledge or wisdom. He asserts that the best gift is the gift of love. Love is the greatest gift. It excels and endures. When all of the other gifts fade away, love is the one that is going to remain. Paul says in 1 Corinthians 13, *"Now abideth faith, hope, love. But the greatest of these is love."* Love is the one thing that is going to last. So, the best thing we can ask from the LORD is for Him to shape our hearts so we can be more loving. Shape our mind, heart and spirit so we can demonstrate *His* kind of love.

Paul shared this with the church of Corinth and talked about what love is. It is kind and patient. But he also talked about what love is not. It is not rude. It is not prideful. Now, by faith, we land on the next phrase that love does not seek its own. Love does not desire its own. Love is not selfish. It is not self-serving. It is not self-absorbed. Love is unselfish. One of the reasons why some of us are selfish is because we are not humble. Humility will help us to be unselfish.

Humility will help us walk in a spirit that seeks not its own. It will help us to have harmony in the house.

One of the things I love about the word of God is it not only gives us principles to practice, but it gives us pictures to perceive. It gives us illustrations, and one of those illustrations of humility is the example and exhortation that the Apostle Paul gives to the church at Philippi. In Philippians, chapter 2, we are not sure what the issue was in the church, but the Apostle Paul was trying to head off a conflict. There were two women in the church named Euodia and Syntyche. They had influence in the church, even if they did not have a title. They had influence and they were self-motivated, self-willed, selfish and self-serving in their service in the church. They were good workers but were self-willed, and there was, apparently, some type of conflict going on. Paul wrote this letter to head off a conflict because these two influential women in the church were about to square off, and people were starting to talk. So, to get ahead of it, Paul wrote this letter to intervene. He wanted to show them that they really needed an attitude adjustment. If they could fix the attitude, then the application would take care of itself.

Paul said in Philippians 2:1-5, *"Therefore if there be any consolation in Christ, if any comfort of love, if any fellowship of the Spirit, if any affection and mercy, fulfill my joy by being like-minded, having the same love, being of one accord, of one mind. Let nothing be done through selfish ambition or conceit, but in lowliness of mind let each esteem others better than himself. Let each of you look out not only for his own interests, but also for the interests of others. Let this mind be in you which was also in Christ Jesus."*

Paul wanted to show the need for harmony in the house through humility in the heart. He gave some reasons for humility, starting in verse one. *"Therefore, if there be any consolation in Christ..."* He first starts out with the word *therefore,* and whenever you see the word *therefore,* it means we just missed something. You need to go back because something was said before that. Before, Paul talked about walking in one mind and one spirit and being unified. Then, he began fleshing out what it means to really walk in unity. When he said if there be any consolation, or if comfort of love, or if any fellowship, or if any affection, that is called a conditional participle. What he really means is *since*. An example would be saying something like, *if there are beaches in Florida*. Well, we know there are beaches in Florida. Or, *if there are amusement parks in Florida*. Well, we know there are amusement parks in Florida. You could replace the words *if there* with the word *since.*

The word consolation that Paul mentioned is a word that means *to call forth*, and it shows the act of what God did for us. God called us to His side, much like a mother who sees her child in danger and calls her child from that dangerous situation to her side. Basically, Paul is saying there was a time in our lives when we were in danger and God called us out of danger. I do not know where you were when He called you, I do not know what you were doing when he called you, but there was something in our lives that we were wrapped up in. That place is where we thought there was no hope until God called us. Maybe that is why the songwriter said, *"I heard the voice of Jesus say, 'Come unto Me and rest; Lay down, O weary one, lay down thy head upon My breast.' I came to Jesus as I was, weary, and worn, and sad; but I found in Him a resting place, and He has made me glad."*

He called me while I was in trouble, and even though I was messed up, He called me. I do not know where you were when God called you, I do not know what you were dealing with when he called you, but I am just glad for the call! You ought to be thankful that in the midst of what you were going through, He called you!

Not only did God call you - this consolation in Christ - but there was some comfort of love. He called us because He loves us with a love that is so deep. It is an unconditional love. He loves me, and He knows me. Even though He knows me - all my faults, all my mess ups, all my shortcomings, everything about me - He still called me, and He still loves me with an everlasting love. He loves me, and He loves you even though you mess up. You may be wrestling in some areas and think that you have strayed so far that God cannot love you. But, you cannot mess up so much that God cannot love you! You cannot go down so far that God cannot love you. You cannot stray so much that God cannot love you. I want you to know God loves you!

Love Unlimited

Jesus says in John 15:9, *"As the father hath loved me, so have I loved you."* He loves me with the same love of the Father. And, what He wants you to do with that love is love one another as He has loved you. In John 13 He says, they will know you are my disciples by how you love one another. That is how they are going to know you belong to Him. Love one another. That is how they are going to know you are a part of Him.

Then, in the book of Matthew, Jesus tells us to love our enemies because that is how love is demonstrated. Some of us love people who love us, and we love people who we like. But, that is not enough. When you have the real love of God, you love your enemies, too. I know you can love people who love you, but Jesus says what good is it to help people who help you? Even the world does that. But, what about you? You are supposed to love your enemies!

In addition to this consolation of Christ, and comfort of love, the Scripture talks about this fellowship of the Spirit. Fellowship means partnership. We are in a partnership. God gave us the Holy Spirit so we could be in partnership. Now ordinarily, when you partner with someone, they usually bring something to the table, and you bring something to the table. For example, if we are in partnership, you are bringing some money, some investment, some networking, some gifts, or even some skills. If I am bringing something, you are bringing something. Paul explained how God partnered with us even though He does not need us. God created us and the world, and even though we were nowhere around when He did so, He still wants to be in fellowship and partnership with us. Look at the goodness of God! We do not bring anything to the table that God does not already possess or can do, but He still wants to partner with us! In partnerships people can be funny and fickle, but God still wants to partner with us.

Philippians 2 continues as it mentions the bowels (affection) and mercy. That word *mercy* means God withholding what we do deserve. He could give us a certain punishment that we deserve, but He does not out of mercy. The prophet Jeremiah said it is because of the LORD's mercies that we are not consumed. It is because of His mercy that we are not wiped out. It is not because we have been so good. It is not because we have dotted every I and crossed every T. It is the mercy of God. And, if we could understand how merciful God has been to us, our attitude would change. If you really understood the love and the mercy of God, you would not stick your nose up so high in the air. You would not look down on people if you understood the mercy of God. God has been good to you!

Based on all we have in common and the reasons for humility outlined in Philippians 2:1 – mercy, love, consolation, He called you, He partnered with you - we ought to walk in humility. In verse 2, it says, *"Fulfill my joy by being like-minded."* In other words, you may have joy, but it is not full joy. The reason it is not full joy is because you are not likeminded with other believers. Some of us get turned off because we want to have our own individual identity. We want to be known for being our own person. But in this Scripture, Paul is saying we ought to be able to agree on the same doctrine and teaching and have the same understanding and agreement.

Some years ago, I taught at the NEXT Conference for Dr. Clifford A. Jones, pastor of Friendship Missionary Baptist Church in Charlotte, North Carolina. It was a church growth and development conference. One of the instructors there was a vice president of Bank of America. The bank's headquarters is in Charlotte. He was there helping churches with finances, and he mentioned one of the issues he was facing at the time. He would give information or instruction to the regional vice presidents, but by the time it got to the district vice presidents and the branch managers who dealt with customers directly, it sometimes changed. As word began to seep down to the local level, it would be altered. To alleviate this problem, they implemented something called a *verbatim*; a script that detailed whatever the vice president or the president needed to communicate. The message is the same all the way down the chain. Everyone gets the same message verbatim, which allows everybody to be on the same page.

What would happen if we had here at Metropolitan NTM Baptist Church a verbatim of spirit? A verbatim of vision? Our vision is to exalt Jesus, equip people, and engage community. That is what we do here. That is what God has given us to accomplish. We are the *light on the hill,* and we are shining that light by exalting, equipping and engaging.

That is our flavor. We are not trying to be like everybody else. We are just trying to do what God has called us to do. You can have two churches right next to each other, and God can give a different vision to each one because He has specific visions for specific churches. Now at the core, all of us ought to be making disciples. That is a general rule for every church and for everybody. But how you carry that out is specific to each particular church, and every auxiliary and leader ought to be in line with the vision of the house.

In Acts 2, all those who were in The Upper Room were on one accord. If you have ever gone to a symphony, you know they have different instruments. Before the concert begins, each musician is tuning up his or her instrument. The sounds are all different. Everyone is playing their own sound, but when the conductor comes out, he hits his baton on the stand. Then, the musicians play in unison and in harmony. That is not the same meaning as the Scripture. Being on one accord means one heart. Our hearts are so united that we not only think alike, we also choose the same doctrine. We are on one accord in our hearts. How awesome it would be if we would be on the same page together; on one accord in our hearts! One mind, one love, and one heart! There is power in unity.

There is a story about a covey of quails. This covey or group of quails were caught in a net, and they were about to be captured in the net. One quail said, *"Wait a minute. I believe we can get out of this if we would all just flap our wings together. If we flapped our wings, we could create enough wind that would lift this net off of us. So, on the count of three, we're going to just flap together and create enough wind to remove this net so we can all be free. Alright, on the count of three: one, two..."* Before he got to three, one of the quails said, *"Wait a minute. First of all, who put you in charge? Second of all, did we vote on this? And third of all, you can't tell us what to do! You ain't our daddy!"* Do you know what happened? They all got captured, and they all died because they chose to flap their lips instead of flapping their wings!

The moral of the story is this. If we are going to accomplish what God wants us to do, we need to stop flapping our lips and start flapping our wings. We need to walk in unity. We need to walk on one accord. Instead of flapping our lips and gums, and let us start flapping our wings together until we can accomplish what God has for us to do. Let us get on one accord with one mind, with one heart, with one spirit, and with one love. Love to do what God wants us to do and love the way He wants us to love.

Let us pray: LORD, by faith, our desire is to be like you. Our desire, LORD is to demonstrate love as you have loved us. LORD, help us to love each other as you have loved us. Help us to even love our enemies as you have loved us. Help us to remove those barriers that prevent love from happening - pride and selfishness, envy, being unkind and impatient. Help us to walk in divine love. Help us to walk in unity. Bring our hearts, our minds, and our spirits together as one. God, we do love you. Thank you for your mercy. God, thank you for your Holy Spirit that abides within us. Help us to walk in your spirit. Help us to walk in love. In Jesus' name, we say hallelujah and amen.

Chapter 8

WALKING IN THE SPIRIT OF LOVE
1 Corinthians 13:4-7 NKJV

"Love suffers long and is kind; love does not envy; love does not parade itself, is not puffed up; does not behave rudely, does not seek its own, is not provoked, thinks no evil; does not rejoice in iniquity, but rejoices in the truth; bears all things, believes all things, hopes all things, endures all things."

The Apostle Paul wrote 1 Corinthians to a young church - the church of Corinth. Members were trying to find their way and place in the church. To their credit, they were extremely gifted. They had many gifts in the church, especially communication gifts such as prophesy and speaking in tongues. In chapter 12, Paul talked about the distribution of these gifts and the rank given to each believer. Because they were given, there was a rank to those gifts. In other words, there is no democracy when it comes to gifts given from the LORD. God gives gifts as God wants to, and He does not need permission from you or me. So do not covet someone else's gift. Do not ever try to be like somebody else. Appreciate the gifts you have because every gift you have is to help the body of Christ. It may not seem as much as this person's gift, or as great as that person's gift may *seem*, but whatever gift God has given you, it is to be used for the kingdom of God. There is a place and purpose for it.

What does God want you to do in the church? What gift has God blessed you with? I am thankful God distributes gifts based on need. Everything Metropolitan Church needs is either here or near. It is either already here or it is very close by because God sends to every local church – just like the church of Corinth - what it needs to fulfill *His* vision for that church.

In addition to the rank, there is also a reach for the gift. At the end of chapter 12, Paul told the church to desire the most helpful gifts. Then, he closes by saying he is going to show them something better than all that – a more excellent way. That is when he begins to talk about love.

In chapter 13, Paul starts out by expounding on the valuelessness of gifts without love. He said, *"Though I speak with the tongues of men and angels, but have not love,"* it means nothing. He can talk like that because he literally heard what angels sound like. In 2 Corinthians 12, he talks about himself in the third person. That is how powerful his experience was. He could not even say, *"I, Paul."* He said he knew a man who went up to the third heaven. He was not even sure if it was in the body or an out of body experience. That is how rhapsodizing his experience was. While he was there in the third heaven, he heard how angels talk. They were using inexpressible words. There are missionaries that have to go in foreign mission fields and have to learn the language, the culture, and the people, while sharing the gospel. Paul said if he did not have to learn at all but could just show up with the great ability to do that - but have not love – he is a zero.

Then Paul said if he gives to the poor one by one, but does not do it in the spirit of love, it profits him nothing. See, you can love without giving, but you cannot give without loving. Therefore, when you give, you ought to do it in the spirit of love. That is why the Bible says when you give, give not grudgingly nor of necessity. Then Paul goes deeper and says if he makes himself – his body – a living sacrifice, but does not have love, it profits him nothing. It is valueless to have gifts without love.

Protect The Spirit of Love

Paul makes an interesting pivot when he changes the narrative in verse 4. He talks about how valuable it is to have love *without* gifts. Everyone has a gift, but even if you did not have a gift and had love, you would still be flowing in the Spirit of God.

Then, he begins to talk about how to walk in the spirit of love. If you are going to walk in the spirit of love, you have to protect the spirit of love. In verse 4, it says, *"Love suffers long and is kind..."* Love is patient. It enables you to forgive when you have been offended and wronged, instead of stirring you to be vengeful; thinking about how you are going to get back at someone.

Why would anyone want to display a love that is patient, long suffering, and kind? The answer is simple. Jesus said in John 15:9, *"As the Father loved Me, I also have loved you."* Then Jesus says in John 13:34-35, As I love you, love one another. I like this because it causes us to look at God's love for us. How many times have we offended God? How many times have we let God down? How many times did He say go left, and we went right? How many times did He say go up, and we went down? How many times have we failed God over and over again, but He keeps on loving us? We have failed Him over and over again, but He keeps on giving to us! We failed Him over and over again, but He keeps on caring for us, extending grace, and extending mercy! And based on God's love for us, we ought to love somebody else.

In Matthew 5:43, Jesus says do not just love one another. He says love your enemies. See, it is easy to love people you like. The world does that! But He says love your enemies. The one that gets on your last nerve! Yes, the one who is on your mind right now! The one you have to look at when you go to work. That family member who you sometimes wonder if you are really related! Are you really in my family? Really? Surely there was a mistake here somewhere down the line!

Practice The Spirit of Love

We also walk in the spirit of love by practicing the spirit of love. Paul outlines this in Galatians 5:22-23 where it says, *"But the fruit of the Spirit is love, joy, peace, longsuffering, kindness, goodness, faithfulness, gentleness, self-control."* So, there are some markers or characteristics of love. We are dealing with a spirit, which means we cannot love that way in our flesh or do it in our own strength and ability. We have to tap into the power of the Holy Spirit. And when we tap into the power of the Holy Spirit, the Spirit of God will love others through us. The Spirit of God will love our enemies through us and will give us the grace to love them. Frankly, we need grace to love some folks whom we do not like. I do not like you, but I have to love you! Admit it. You are not happy to see everybody who comes to the family reunion!

In 1 Corinthians 13:4, Paul gives some more characteristics of love, which teaches us how to practice love. He says, *"Love does not envy, love does not parade itself, is not puffed up; does not behave rudely, does not seek its own, is not provoked, thinks no evil; does not rejoice in iniquity, but rejoices in the truth."* He gives here, along with the first two – patience and kindness – 15 verbs to describe love. Two sevens plus one. Seven in the Bible is a number of perfection and completeness. One is the number of wholeness. He gives seven, seven, plus one. Two completeness, perfection and wholeness. He said I am going to give you a list of what love looks like. I am going to describe to you how to love.

So, does love envy? No. Never. The word envy does not just mean I want your house or car. It means, I do not even want you to have it. Does love parade itself? Is it puffed up? No. Never. Puffed up means to be filled with hot air. Love is not walking around thinking you are better than other people. Love does not do that. Does love behave rudely? No. Never. I do not look for opportunities to embarrass people. Does it seek its own? No. Never. Someone should go to the people in Corinth over in chapter 6 who are going to pagans and suing one another and tell them that love does not seek its own. Someone needs to go tell them in chapters 8, 9, and 10 who are eating meat that was sacrificed to idols but has become a stumbling block to immature believers that love does not seek its own. No. Never. Is it provoked? Does it think evil? No. Never. Does it keep a record of wrongs? A ledger of what somebody did to you so that you can then plan your revenge? No. Never. Does it rejoice in iniquity? No. Never. It rejoices in the truth. That means, when I see someone else fall or make a mistake, I do not laugh at them. I pray for them. I learn from them, but I do not laugh at them. Whatever you see someone else do, you may do too, given the same circumstances and frame of mind. Them today, you tomorrow. Be careful how you laugh at people who mess up. Behavior follows belief. If you say you believe in love and believe in God, there ought to be some kind of sign.

Preserve The Spirit of Love

If we are going to walk in the spirit of love we also have to preserve the spirit of love. 1 Corinthians 13:7 says, love *"bears all things, believes all things, hopes all things, endures all things."* The first quadrant in this four-fold description of love says it bears all things. That means, when

Love Unlimited

I see my brother slipping, I do not expose him. I cover him. Not only does it bear all things, it hopes all things. When I hear something about my brother, I hope it is not true. I do not go on a fishing exposition. I hope it is not true. But, perhaps you find out it is true. Then you believe all things. Because I believe it can get better. I believe this may be a slip up, but it is not who he is or she is. It may be a season, but I believe he or she is better than that. Now, what if they still disappoint my belief? I endure it. I leave it in the LORD's hands. I have an issue, though. How am I going to do that? How can I preserve that type of love? Wait a minute. God has loved me. And God has loved me with an everlasting love. God has loved me in such a way that even though I mess up, nothing can separate me from the love of God in Christ Jesus. The Apostle Paul says in Romans 8:35-39, *"Who shall separate us from the love of Christ? Shall tribulation, or distress, or persecution, or famine, or nakedness, or peril, or sword?" "...We are accounted as sheep for the slaughter. Yet in all these things we are more than conquerors through Him who loved us. For I am persuaded, that neither death, nor life, nor angels, nor principalities, nor powers, nor things present nor things to come, nor height, nor depth, nor any other created thing, shall be able to separate us from the love of God which is in Christ Jesus our Lord."*

I love God because He first loved me. Oh, how I love Jesus because He first loved me. Is there anyone who is thankful for His love? Nothing will separate us. Trouble will not do it. Heartache will not do it. Be thankful for the love of God.

Love Unlimited

Some friends may not love you. Some family members may not love you, but He loves you!

Let us pray: Heavenly Father, thank you for loving us even when we have failed you. Thank you for showing us the value of love and how to love. Help us to always walk in the spirit of love. Help us to practice it each day when we encounter our brothers and sisters. In Jesus' name, we pray. Amen.

Chapter 9

LOVE NEVER FAILS
1 Corinthians 13:8-10 NKJV

"Love never fails. But whether there are prophecies, they will fail; whether there are tongues, they will cease; whether there is knowledge, it will vanish away. For we know in part and we prophesy in part. But when that which is perfect has come, then that which is in part will be done away."

When people travel to different cities, there are certain sites and attractions they make sure they visit. If you go to Paris, you would likely go to the Louvre Museum or the Eiffel Tower. If you go to Washington, DC, you would likely go to the King Memorial, the Jefferson Memorial, or the African American Museum. If you go to New York City, you might want to see the Statue of Liberty, the United Nations, or the Empire State Building. But when you go to the New Testament, there is one chapter people are drawn and attracted to. That is chapter 13 of 1 Corinthians. Much like the 23rd Psalm of the Old Testament, chapter 13 of 1 Corinthians in the New Testament draws, attracts and ministers to us in powerful ways.

It is an unusual letter in this chapter, because it is a letter of correction and judgement. Right in the center of this letter is a beautiful expression and explanation on love. The church of Corinth was a church that was mastered by materialism. As I mentioned before, they were self-serving, self-absorbed and selfish. God could not do much through them because they resisted and rejected the power and strength of the Holy Spirit. So, the Apostle Paul started writing to them in a way they could understand. God really wanted to reach the city of Corinth through the church of Corinth. That is why He had that church established. But, He could not do it because they rejected and resisted the things of God. They had gifts, talents and skills, but they were so self-absorbed, God could not do much through them. Instead of the church being able to reach the city of Corinth, Corinth was reaching the church. Just like a ship in water, it is ok when a ship is in the water, but you have a problem when the water gets into the ship.

Love Has an Enduring Quality

In the middle of this letter, the Apostle Paul tried explaining to the Corinthians what love was and how important it was for them to show love to people who were proclaiming Christ as their Savior and Redeemer. The people were desiring gifts, but by now you ought to know that the best gift is the gift of love. If you really want to desire a great gift, desire love. They were caught up in the gift of tongues, prophesy and knowledge. All those gifts are fine. But the problem is, all those gifts will pass away. They are here for a reason and a season. But, the gift of love is going to last forever. So, if you want to desire a gift, desire the best gift.

Paul further emphasized this point by explaining to them that love will never fail. Spiritual gifts will fail, fall and fade. But the gift of love will last forever. Why is it that love never fails? What is it about love that does not fade away? The answer is simple. Love has an enduring quality. Chapter 13 talks about the enduring quality of love. Paul said love will last forever. It never ends. There is never a time when love is not appropriate. Love is always the right approach. It is always relevant and permanent because love never fails. Prophesies will cease. They are here for a season and gone for a season. Love lasts forever. Real godly love – the agape love that the New Testament talks about – is not on and off. When you do not love someone today, then you love them tomorrow, that is not a God-kind of love. Love is consistent. Love is enduring. Love keeps going. Paul said tongues will cease. They will be stilled. Love is never still in the face of need.

Paul said knowledge will fade away, but love will keep going. Even when our bodies pass away, love will keep going. Because nothing will separate us from the love of God. Not even death. Prophesies will cease. What is prophesy? It is the supernatural ability to speak God's word – the truth of God – in a situation, regardless of the consequences. We need prophesy now. We need those who will boldly declare God's word and not care what people think. God told the Prophet Jeremiah to not be afraid of their faces. Stand boldly and declare God's words. I cannot stand it when a preacher is scared to declare the word. If God has called you to preach it, do not care about what people say. Leave the consequences up to Him, and declare His word boldly. But, there will come a time when prophesy will fade. We will not need prophesy because God is the fulfillment of prophesy.

Gifts are temporal, but God is permanent. Look at the gift of speaking in tongues. Tongues are the supernatural ability to speak in a language you have not been taught, whether it is a heavenly language or earthly language. In chapter 14, Paul said tongues are to build the believer and build the church. When it is to build the church, there is an interpreter. When it is to build you, it is a language that lifts you up and edifies you. Paul said, *"I speak with tongues more than you all; yet in the church I would rather speak five words with my understanding, that I may teach others also, than ten thousand words in a tongue,"* because tongues are going to cease.

There will come a time when knowledge will also cease. Knowledge is the distinct spiritual ability to seek, gather, organize, and clarify facts and ideas on a number of subjects to share them with someone. But even knowledge will cease. You will not need knowledge. Man needs prophesy, tongues and knowledge. God does not need prophesy because He is the fulfillment of prophesy. He does not need tongues. God does not need knowledge because He knows everything. He is omniscient. There will come a time when we will not need prophesy, tongues or knowledge.

Not only are these gifts passing, but they are incomplete. In 1 Corinthians 13:9, it says, *"For we know in part and we prophesy in part."* So, they are incomplete. That is not the end of it. There will come a time when that which is perfect (God) comes. And that which is part will be done away with. Paul's point is this. The Corinthians were caught up in gifts and temporal things. He was trying to move them to something that was permanent and would not fade. Get into grace. That is love. Love is always appropriate. Sometimes, telling folks how much you know is not appropriate. Or, you trying to get someone straight is not appropriate. Even if you are right, you can win the argument and lose a person. It is about love, because love is always appropriate. Love can outlast anything. It is the one thing that will always stand when everything else has fallen. When your family fades and your friends turn their backs on you, you can always depend on the love of God.

Love Unlimited

The great R&B singer, Rick James, wrote some hit songs: "Ebony Eyes", "Fire and Desire", and my favorite – "Super Freak". *"She was a very naughty girl. The kind you don't take home to mother!"* I was reading up on Rick James one day and realized that song writers and producers get royalties. If they play your song on the radio, in the movies, or on commercials, you get royalties from that. They get them quarterly. Unfortunately, Rick James had a substance abuse issue and would spend up all of his money on drugs and women and would go broke. When he would lose all his money, he would go to the mailbox and get checks for $25,000, $50,000, $100,000 - depending on how often his songs were used. And when he would mess that up, he would go back to the mailbox the following quarter to get more money. This happened year after year. His royalty checks would never run out. Because as long as they played his songs and used his music, he got a royalty check. If the royalty checks from "Super Freak" did not run out, how much more would the love from a super God not run out? You cannot exhaust or suspend the love of God because His love never fails!

Love Has an Encouraging Quality

Love does not fail because love is desiring the best for someone. The New Testament concept of love says I want the best for you. Love is a volitional, willful desire to want the best. It is not based on how I feel or if I want to do it. Love, whether I feel like it or not, always wants the best for you. Love does not mean I am somebody's doormat, though. Love does not mean you can say anything to me and treat me any kind of way, while I sit there and take it. Sometimes, love is confrontation. Sometimes, it is correction. Sometimes, it is giving direction and discipline. Sometimes, it is tough love. Sometimes, it is saying no because I want the best for you. And if I want the best for you, I do not always give in to everything you say. That is not love. Sometimes, I have to say no and let you stand on your own two feet instead of helping you out over and over again. Because if I keep enabling you, you will never reach your best.

Sometimes, we just do not have the capacity to love. That is why we need to understand love is a fruit of the Spirit, not just a gift. Galatians 5:22 says, *"And the fruit of the spirit is love."* Paul names nine fruits of the Spirit, but love is the first one because all of the other ones grow out of love. We need to submit ourselves under the control of the Holy Spirit and allow the Holy Spirit to fill us. We need to allow the Holy Spirit to aide and empower us because there are times when we may not feel like being loving, but God, through His spirit, can love through us. Romans 5:5 says, *"...The love of God has been poured out in our hearts by the Holy Spirit who was given to us."*

Hurricane Beryl swept through Houston in 2024. More than 2 million homes and businesses were without electricity. I watched news coverage from Houston's Channel 13 as it was reporting from the Houston Medical Center. I was concerned about the millions of homes and businesses without power and wondered about those in the hospitals. They reported that the hospital never lost power in the midst of the storm. It wasn't that the hurricane did not come through, but the hospital had backup generators, so when the electricity stopped working in Houston, there were things in place that helped the electricity continue, even when the power ran out. The Holy Spirit is *your* backup generator. When your power and ability run out, you can tap into the Holy Spirit and keep on loving, giving and serving, not in your own strength, but in the strength of the Holy Spirit!

Love Unlimited

Love Has an Exalting Quality

So far in this chapter, I have expounded on the need and priority of love and how valueless it is to have gifts without grace, as Paul outlined in verses 1-3. *Though I speak with the tongues of men and angels, but have not love, it means nothing. Though I give to the poor and give myself to the poor, without love, it profits me nothing.* Then, I outlined the prerogative of love that Paul mentioned in verses 4-7 when he gave 15 qualities of what love is. Now, I want to dive into the permanence of love.

Love never fails. You cannot improve on love. Paul is not talking about the success or failure of love. He is talking about the essence of love. You cannot improve on it because it never loses its value. Love is *always* willing to suffer long. It is *always* kind. Love *never* envies. It *never* parades itself, is *never* puffed up, *never* behaves rudely, *never* seeks its own, is *never* provoked, *never* thinks evil, *never* rejoices in iniquity. Love *always* bears all things, love *always* believes all things, love *always* hopes all things, and *always* endures all things. It never fails.

Human love may fade and fail, but God's love never runs out. And, I am thankful for God's love. If you want to know about the love of Christ, look at the fact that it was God who loved us so much that He went to a hill called Calvary. They put Him on a cross with six-inch nails in His hands and nine-foot rivets in His feet. They put a spear in His side and a crown of thorns on His head. But, why did He endure all of that? Not because He had to, but because He loved us. He told Pilot He could have called 10,000 angels, but because of His love for us, He died. They hung Him high and stretched Him wide. That is what love is. Jesus went to Calvary to save a wrench like you and me. That's love. But that's not how the story ends. Three days later, He rose again. That's love. God will always be there for us. When family and friends' love is gone, God will keep on loving us. *"What will separate us from the love of Jesus Christ? Should tribulation, or distress, or persecution, or famine, or nakedness, or peril, or sword?"* The answer is in Romans 8:38. *"For I am persuaded that neither death nor life, nor angels nor principalities nor powers, nor things present nor things to come, nor height nor depth, nor any other created thing, shall be able to separate us from the love of God which is in Christ Jesus our Lord."*

Are you thankful and grateful for His love? His love wakes you up every morning. It gives you strength, joy and peace. Because of His love, we should give Him glory and praise. Because of His love, I will bless the LORD at all times, and His praise shall continually be in my mouth. My soul will make her boast in the Lord. The humble will hear their own and be glad. For God so loved the world that He gave His only begotten son, and whosoever believe in Him should not perish, but have everlasting life. I thank God for His love. For God commended His love toward us that while we were yet sinners, while I was going in the wrong direction, while I was too mean to live but not ready to die, He died for me! We all ought to be grateful for His love!

"I was sinking deep in sin, far from the peaceful shore very deeply stained within, sinking to rise no more. But the master of the sea heard my despairing cry. From the waters lifted me, now safe am I. Love lifted me. Love lifted me. And when nothing else could help, love lifted me."

Let us pray: Dear God, thank you for teaching us that the best gift is the gift of love. Not only is it a gift, but a fruit of the Spirit. Help

Love Unlimited

us to submit ourselves under the control of the Holy Spirit when we may not feel like being loving. We know that love never fails, and we are so thankful to you for that. In Jesus' name we pray, Amen.

Love Unlimited

Chapter 10

I'M GROWING UP
1 Corinthians 13:11-13 NKJV

"When I was a child, I spoke as a child, I understood as a child, I thought as a child; but when I became a man, I put away childish things. For now we see in a mirror, dimly, but then face to face. Now I know in part, but then I shall know just as I also am known. And now abide faith, hope, love, these three; but the greatest of these is love."

If we are not careful, we will spend our time criticizing, copying, and coveting other people's gifts without being creative in the gifts we have. If you are a parent with more than one child, perhaps you have experienced your children going downstairs on Christmas Day and seeing all the gifts you have for them. One starts opening a gift with excitement and begins playing with that toy. There are so many gifts that he will put that one aside to open more. He will not think about that toy anymore until another child starts to play with it. Then, all of a sudden, he wants to play with it again. He was not thinking about the toy before, but now he wants to play with it again.

That is how many of us are with our spiritual gifts. So many of the gifts we have lie dormant. They are not discovered, developed or demonstrated. But we watch what other people do and how they operate in their spiritual gifts. And

if we are not careful, we will criticize it, covet it, or even try to copy it. What we ought to do is just be creative in the gift God has given us because God has given everyone a particular spiritual gift that He wants us to use to build up the church; the body of Christ.

God gave gifts, and the Apostle Paul shared with the church of Corinth how it was important to use those gifts. This was a church that had gifts but no grace. They had talent but were not connected to the truth. They became very arrogant and insulated. It became all about them and never about other people. He wanted to show a more excellent way. No matter what gift they were operating in, they were to operate in the spirit of love. He closes our Scripture focus on the permanency of love. Love will last when all the gifts leave. When tongues are finished, when knowledge is finished, when prophecy is done, you still need love.

Mature In Your Person

Why did God give us spiritual gifts? He has given gifts to help us on our journey. God has given *you* a gift to mature you in your person. Verse 11 says, *"When I was a child, I spoke as a child, I understood as a child, I thought as a child; but when I became a man, I put away childish things."* God is more concerned about your growth than your comfort. God is not overly concerned about how good you feel and how comfortable you are. God is concerned about your spiritual growth. 2 Peter 3:18 says, *"But grow in the grace and knowledge of our Lord and Savior Jesus Christ."* God wants us to grow. Something is wrong if the same stuff that tripped you up last year, is tripping you up this year. You do not have to be perfect. It is not about perfection, but progress. You ought to be a little further down the line this year than you were last year. The same baby faith you had last year, you should be a little more mature now. And, God is not in the habit of promoting spiritual brats!

He said I have planted you and watered you with the word. And now it is time for you to grow and develop. If we are not growing, sometimes God will send us through seasons of suffering and periods of pain to help us grow. Because some of us do not grow when things are going well, but only under heat and the endurance of patience. Patience will help you endure. If you are going through problems and issues and are wondering why, it could be because God is saying it is time for you to grow up.

Here is a quick test to determine if you are growing. In 1 Corinthians 13:4, put your name in verse 4 and see if it applies to you. I will put my name in. Damone suffers long and is kind. Damone does not envy. Damone does not parade himself. Damone is not puffed up. Damone does not behave rudely. Damone does not seek his own kind. Damone is not provoked. Damone thinks no evil. Damone does not rejoice in iniquity, but rejoices in the truth. Damone bears all things, believes all things, hopes all things, endures all things. Can you put your name there?

We need to be growing. That is what Jesus did. In Luke 2:52, it says, *"And Jesus increased in wisdom and stature, and in favor with God and men."* Once you start growing spiritually, then you start growing in other areas in your life — personally, relationally, and socially. When it says Jesus grew, of course the Scripture is talking about the human side of Him. God is God. He is the same yesterday and today and forevermore. God cannot grow, but the human aspect of Jesus grew and increased in wisdom. His mental development grew and the grace of God was upon Him. This is not referring to saving and redeeming grace. Jesus did not need to be rescued from sin by grace because He was sinless. But this is referring to the favor and blessing of God that was upon Him. The love that was lavished upon Him. Just like Jesus grew, we need to grow. We need to grow in knowledge and wisdom. Knowledge is information and wisdom is how to apply that knowledge. We can have a lot of knowledge, but if we do not have wisdom to go with it, it is not going to help us grow. Proverbs 4:5 says, *"Get wisdom! Get understanding! Do not forget, nor turn away from the words of my mouth. Do not forsake her, and she will preserve you; Love her, and she will keep you."* Verse 8 says, *"Exalt her, and she will promote you. She will bring you honor, when you embrace her."* You should be always seeking to improve yourself.

I have been preaching for 30 years. I have been in pastoral ministry for 24 of those years. Three years, I was the assistant pastor at Ebenezar Baptist Church in Indianapolis, Indiana and the senior pastor at Metropolitan New

Love Unlimited

Testament Missionary Baptist Church in Albany, New York for 21 years. And, I am still growing. I still have room to grow. I love preaching and teaching. Last year, I *taught* a group on preaching for Dr. Jesse Bottoms, pastor of Beulah Baptist Church in Poughkeepsie, New York. The week after that, I *took* a class on preaching. I am never at a point that I think I cannot learn something. I am never at a point where I cannot develop and hone my skills and be better. So, as I am sharing information, I still need to sit at somebody's feet and get some information to help me grow and develop. I have not reached it all, and neither have you.

What are you doing to grow yourself if you want to make yourself more marketable. It may mean getting a new skill set or taking another class. So, when the next promotion comes, they can consider you and not look over you. Everyone has to go through some growth. Teachers have to go through professional development. Doctors have to learn new procedures. Lawyers have to understand new laws that have changed. What are you doing to grow yourself? Or, do you think you have reached it? Some may say, *"Well, you know you can't teach an old dog new tricks!"* Well, you are not a dog, and these are not tricks!

As you begin to grow personally, the church begins to grow. As the church grows, the church also needs to grow up. We need to be maturing. That is the purpose of a pastor's spiritual gift. It is not just to make you feel good, but to help you grow. Ephesians 4:11 says, *"And he Himself gave some to be apostles, some prophets, some evangelists, and some pastors and teachers, for the equipping of the saints for the work of ministry, for the edifying of the body of Christ, till we all come to the unity of the faith and of the knowledge of the Son of God, to a perfect man, to the measure of the stature of the fullness of Christ; that we should no longer be children [child-like, spiritual babies, spoiled brats], tossed to and fro and carried about with every wind of doctrine, by the trickery of men, in the cunning craftiness of deceitful plotting, but, speaking the truth in love, may grow up in all things into Him who is the head-Christ."*

You should be growing, developing and using your gifts, so that you do not see the church just as somewhere you go to receive. When you grow up, then you will understand it is not about what you can get from the church, but about what you can share. It is not about what the church can do or has not done for you. Have you ever asked what you have done for the church or what you are doing? Are you giving your time, your talent, your treasure, or your testimony? Are you promoting the church? For ministry leaders, how many people have joined your ministry this year? If you are over a ministry, has your ministry grown? If you are a ministry leader and no one has joined, or you are not doing anything to develop yourself or your membership, something is wrong. What steps are you taking to grow your ministry? Not only should you be growing, but the church should be growing too.

Manage Perplexity

God has given us spiritual gifts to manage our perplexities. 1 Corinthians 13:12 says, *"For now we see in a mirror, dimly, but then face to face. Now I know in part, but then I shall know just as I also am known."* There were no glass windows in those days when the Scriptures were written. They had a crude kind of glass but was not used for windows. Sometimes, they were transparent crystals. But most of the time, they would use brass. It was a dim brass, not something clear. They would try to see an image, but could only see it dimly. Sometimes, that is how life is. We are looking through life like a dim glass or brass that we cannot see clearly. That is why we need the gift of discernment. If not, we will get so caught up in the container – the outside – that we miss the content on the inside. Some people have done that to you. They saw through a glass dimly. Because you did not match how they thought you should look, or the background they thought you should have, or the color they thought you should be, or the gender they thought you should be, they never got around to the content because they were so caught up in the container. Sometimes, we see through the glass dimly ourselves. How many people have you ignored or drawn conclusions about because you were looking on the outside and they did not match what you thought they should be? You never got around to the content because you were looking at the container and seeing through a glass dimly. That is why in relationships you cannot just get caught up solely on what you see on the outside. You can be fascinated by the container, then when you get home, you may realize there is no content in the container.

We see through a glass dimly. Walking through life is not always clear. We know in part, but we do not always know all things. Although we know somethings and are blessed by revelation through God's word, there is still some unanswered questions. There are still some things we do not all together comprehend. We see through a glass dimly, and that is why we need to exercise faith. Because we walk by faith and not by sight. We cannot just walk by sight because we see through a glass dimly. We cannot see, understand or perceive it all. It is too fuzzy. So, we have to walk with faith. God gives us faith, and when we cannot see it with our eyes, at least we know and understand He is helping us walk through it.

Have you ever walked through the house with a night light? The night light is not as bright as the regular light, but it is bright enough to help you through the dark. And that is what faith is. Faith is like your night light. It may not be as bright as you want it, but your faith will get you through darkness. Has God ever sent you through some dark times and moments? It was not all you wanted it to be, but it got you through. While you are waiting for God to come through, waiting on the manifestation, or waiting on deliverance, you still have a light that says, *"I know you're going to do it, Jesus. I know you are going to come through for me!"*

Love Unlimited

When you are seeing through a glass dimly, you have to learn how to negotiate your *now*. *Now*, we see through a glass dimly, *then* face to face. *Now*, I know in part, but *then* I shall know just as I also am known. *Now*, abide faith hope and love. You have to learn how to negotiate the *now* because some of you are between the *now* and *then*. *Now*, I have some issues, and *now* I have some problems and burdens, but I am waiting on my *then*, which is when the blessings come. I am waiting on God to come through. I am between the *almost*, and the *not yet*. You are praying for it to happen, and it has not happened yet. That is where some of you are. Life will make you negotiate your *now*. I do not know how to make it yet because I am trying to get through my *now* to *then*. You need to learn how to negotiate the *now*.

If you know my testimony, you know I have dyslexia. It is just a different form of learning. I have had it all my life. Sometimes, people would make me think I was not smart enough. I was put in special classes. But, thank God I had a mother who helped me understand who I was. She shared with me other successful people who also had dyslexia. Charles Schwab, the financier; Andraé Crouch, the great gospel singer; and three different US presidents have had dyslexia. My mother said, *"Damone, there is no excuse for any kind of failure. If they can succeed, you can succeed. If they can make it, you can make it."*

One of the things about dyslexia is it causes you to see things backwards. It causes you to see things differently. It could be a word or a phrase. For illustration purposes, I want to give you permission to be dyslexic. I want you to see this backwards. Look at the word *now*. If you are wondering how you are going to make it *now*, shift the n-o-w to w-o-n. It says won! Sometimes, when you are going through trouble, you have to be dyslexic. You have to see things differently. It is *not* now I am sick, or now I am having financial problems, or now I cannot make it. It is won! I already have the victory. I am already more than a conqueror. I already have the manifestation. I am already a champion even before it happens. I do not have to wait until the battle is over. I can shout now because I know I have already won! It may not look like it, but you have already won, even if you cannot see it yet. Just wait on the LORD and be of good courage. He will strengthen your heart. *"They that wait upon the LORD shall renew their strength; they shall mount up with wings as eagles; they shall run, and not be weary; and they shall walk, and not faint."*

Do not wait until your breakthrough happens. You have to see it by faith. When you see it by faith, you do not have to wait to praise God. You can praise and bless Him right now!

Let us pray: LORD, we thank you for victory right now. We thank you for comfort. Thank you for deliverance. Thank you for financial breakthrough, thank you for protection over our children, over our grandchildren, and over our nieces and nephews. Thank you for all the gifts you have given us. Help us to grow and mature individually and as the body of Christ. In Jesus' name. Hallelujah and amen.

Chapter 11

Personal Spiritual Journey on Love
Mark 5:25-29 NKJV

"Now a certain woman had a flow of blood for twelve years, and had suffered many things from many physicians. She had spent all that she had and was no better, but rather grew worse. When she heard about Jesus, she came behind Him in the crowd and touched His garment. For she said, 'If only I may touch His clothes, I shall be made well.' Immediately the fountain of her blood was dried up, and she felt in her body that she was healed of the affliction."

Faith In Action

This story about the unnamed woman with an issue of blood in the book of Mark is a familiar one. I have been preaching since 2003, and I have expounded on this text from the pulpit many times. Any good preacher would. It is a miraculous story in the Bible that exemplifies Jesus' healing powers. At the center of this healing was the woman's faith. We may not know her name – that is not even important in this lesson – but we know she had enough sense to recognize the extent of Jesus' power. She went from doctor to doctor to get relief after suffering from a bleed for 12 years.

Broke and still sick, the woman believed she would be healed by merely touching the clothes Jesus had on. There was something about the garment of Jesus. You know how a woman prances around in her boyfriend's jersey after he has worn it because it has a certain energy or smell that reminds her of him or cheers her up? Or how about when you take an old shirt of a loved one and turn it into a pillow keepsake after someone transitions? That pillow brings comfort to the one left to cherish the memories. Well, this desire to touch Jesus' clothes was beyond mere comfort and memories. This lady was broke, bleeding and bold enough to belief something transformative would happen if she could get to Him. She had nothing to lose and everything to gain.

I am sure she heard about Jesus healing a man with an unclean spirit. Maybe she heard about Jesus healing a man with a withered hand in the synagogue. Or, maybe she heard about Jesus healing a paralyzed man in Capernaum. Whatever it was, this was personal for her. She was in dire need of a physical healing because she had gone to all the doctors she could, but it yielded no relief. However, she knew if she could push past the crowd and make her way to Jesus, she would finally be healed. This was faith in action, and it came with a reward. In verse 34, Jesus said, *"Daughter, your faith has made you well. Go in peace, and be healed of your affliction."*

Serving and Suffering

As many times as I have preached this story before, it has never felt more personal and timelier as it has recently. For the past 4 years, I have been dealing with different levels of pain in my body. It came to a head in April 2023. My doctor misdiagnosed my condition, convincing me that it was sciatica. There was an impingement mobility in my nerve which affected my left leg. It was very painful and not getting any better. There were days where I would fall to the ground. My knees would just buckle, and I would fall unexpectedly. As you can imagine, that was pretty scary.

I was receiving physical therapy in June 2023, and I was able to stand with no problem. By August, it was a different picture. I could not even stand. It had gotten so bad, I had to take two months off from my role as senior pastor, as advised by my doctor. This was something I had never done in all my years of preaching. I returned to the church in November. I had been resting at home but not getting any better. I came back to the church weaker, not stronger. I went from walking with a stick, to walking with a cane, to walking with a walker. Then, I saw a neurologist who also misdiagnosed me. There was a time when I would have two or three doctor's appointments a week. This was extremely frustrating. Just like the woman with an issue of blood in the book of Mark, I saw many doctors, but I was getting worse. In addition to the falling and lack of mobility, I was in a lot of pain in my legs and upper body. In December, I had lots of blood work done, multiple MRIs, and still no relief.

Physically, it had gotten so bad that I was not able to climb the stairs at home. I did not have the strength. When I went to church, it would take a few men to help get me out of the car and into the building.

There were some rough days when I was in so much pain. It is indescribable. The pain was debilitating. I went from one bed to another and from couch to chair, just to find comfort. My wife would massage the painful area to bring some relief. That would help temporarily, but the pain would come back when she would stop. I was on a lot of medication to neutralize the pain. I would listen to gospel music, pray, and read Scriptures for encouragement.

See, pastors and spiritual leaders have to appear strong to their congregation. The people depend on *us* to help them get through *their* situations. I would put on a pretty good front around people. But I was serving and suffering. I tried to hide it the best I could.

Spiritual Warfare

After really examining what was going on, it hit me. This was not just physical; it was spiritual warfare. It was a satanic attack. So, my whole approach and prayer life shifted. I have a mentor, Dr. Clifford A. Jones, who pastors Friendship Baptist Church in Charlotte, North Carolina. He would reach out to me weekly while I was going through. One day, he asked me if I was scared. I said no. He asked me if I was worried. I said no, but I was growing impatient in this process. He said, *"You know the process is not going to go any faster because you are impatient, right?"* This felt like a

Love Unlimited

Job experience. Job was a righteous and godly man from Uz. Even he suffered and was frustrated with his suffering. Dr. Jones encouraged me to listen to God. Because this situation was spiritual, I had to deal with it spiritually. The funny thing is, the doctors did a lot of bloodwork but the results did not show anything. It only ruled out what they were looking for. It was not Lou Gehrig's disease. It was not cancer. They did not know what it was, only what it was not. That is because this was not just physical. It was spiritual. So, my prayer life changed. My study time changed. Before all this, I studied to prepare a lesson, Bible study, or a sermon. But at this time, it was because I needed God to speak to me, and God speaks to me through His word. I would study an average of 25 hours per week prior to this experience, but I increased it. I needed the word to speak to Damone. I was after God for something, and I had to go after Him in a way that I had never gone after Him before.

In January 2024, I saw a podiatrist. He said there was nothing wrong with my legs or feet, but something was wrong with my nerves. He suggested I get out of Albany to find out what it was. That was on a Tuesday. By Friday, I saw my rehab doctor again. He told me he had a friend who is a neuromuscular doctor in Rochester, New York, but it would take about six months to see him. Then, I prayed for God to send me to someone who had the knowledge to know what was going on. I googled top neuromuscular doctors in New York City. The doctor that I ultimately chose was on that list. She was in the top five in NYC. So, I called her office that Friday afternoon and talked to her secretary. I asked, *"Do you think this doctor will be able to figure out what's wrong with me?"* She said, *"Sir, there have been patients who have come in here because the other doctors couldn't figure out what was wrong. But, she figured it out. I'm not saying that because I work for her. I'm saying it because it is the truth."* So, I asked how soon could I see her. She said, *"Funny you should ask. I just got a cancellation for next Friday."* I gladly took that appointment. My wife and I immediately booked a train to Manhattan.

When the doctor examined me during the appointment, she had me walk up and down the hall. I was holding on to the wall for fear of falling. Then she said, *"I think I know what's wrong with you, but we need to run some tests to confirm."* Finally! I had a diagnosis and a plan of action, but I had to get regular treatments. The doctor said, *"With the treatment, strength training, physical therapy, perseverance, and patience, you should improve."* I would also add prayer to that list. After only two weeks of treatments, I saw an improvement. I was on a walker, and at home I would grab the wall to get from the bedroom to the bathroom down the hall. But one day, I realized I was hobbling through without assistance! It has been a year now. I am very much still going through the healing process because this condition affects my nerves. The nervous system is the slowest system in the body to heal. Those nerves and muscles that are the furthest from the spine – those in the feet, hands and fingers - take the longest. Healing takes time, but I am on the road to be healed.

Faith Model

While going through this whole ordeal, I did a lot of listening to God. In those still moments, I was really trying to hear from Him. *"What am I to learn from this?"* I wondered. *"What am I to gain from this?"* I cannot count the number of trips I took to urgent care and the emergency room. When I would go and they would find out that I am a pastor leading a flock here in Albany and abroad with our live streaming, two or three doctors would tell me, *"Oh wow, you are going to see a lot of people come to your church because you are going to be a faith model!"* Interestingly, I had been teaching about model faith, and this experience has made me realize that people needed to see it. They needed to see *me* go through it. Faith leaders often feel the need to be strong. People draw strength from us. But, I am convinced the people needed to see me weather this storm.

This experience altered the way I do church. I could only stand for about seven minutes, so my doctor recommended I do not stand while preaching. I started preaching while sitting in a chair. The church adjusted to it. It was not about my posture anyway. It was about the word.

This experience also affected me financially. My specialized doctor was out of network. The traveling. The co-pays. The NYC hotel stays. But, what could I do? I had to pay for a good quality of life. It had to be done if I wanted the right care and if I wanted to get well. You definitely get what you pay for.

Love In the Midst of Pain

God demonstrates His love in different ways. It is not always through what we would consider positive, good or enjoyable experiences. Oftentimes, it is through seasons of pain, suffering and heartache. When God works out situations in our lives, we know for sure that His hand is in all of it. It reminds me of the book of Esther. It is the only book of the Bible where God's name is not mentioned, yet we see evidence of Him all throughout.

I am just grateful to God for the healthcare team I ultimately had. My doctor was great. She called me regularly to check on me, and she was extremely thorough. The physical therapist actually specialized in this particular ailment, so he was very knowledgeable. One of the physical therapists I worked with had a father who suffered from the same thing, so he saw it on both ends – personal and professional. My rehab doctor was good, too. They were all absolutely amazing, working in collaboration with one another and letting me know exactly what I needed to do.

The support from my church, Metropolitan New Testament Mission Baptist Church, has been absolutely amazing. Priceless. I cannot put a number on the prayers, text messages, gifts, and unexpected acts of kindness. The outpouring of support has been phenomenal. It was good and bad at the same time. What do I mean by that? Well, when I was going through this period of illness, the city of Albany named a street after me because of my service in the community for 20 years, the same street that Metropolitan is on. How awesome is that? But, while I was being celebrated, I could not walk. I was seated on a chair. It was a celebration and struggle all at the same time. Yet, God was loving me through it all.

Dr. Boahema Pinto-Smith, a member of Metropolitan, was outstanding during my time of need. She is an emergency room doctor at Albany Medical Center, and she and her husband just happen to be long-time members of the church. God demonstrated His love for me through her as well. I could reach out to her at any time. She would guide me through the medical jargon and break down information for me to make it easily understood. It was good to have a doctor I could call and share information with. I was not her patient. I was her pastor. This was not her area of expertise, but I could send her MRI results, and she would send my info to other doctors in her network to gather additional information.

God demonstrated His love through timing. I saw divine prearrangements. To be able to see my doctor within a week when sometimes it takes three months was all God. Then, I began to see improvements two weeks into my treatments, even though the doctor said it would take about eight weeks.

God demonstrated His love by allowing me to go through, allowing my faith to be strengthened, and allowing me to see the love of my wife, my family, and friends around the country and locally. God truly loved me through them.

Love Unlimited

God has stretched my faith and stretched my love. I have a different sensitivity to those who go through physical ailments. People have always sought me to pray for their healing. And, I have always obliged. But it is different now. Because I, too, know that in these difficult moments, your confidence in the face of adversity and resolve is questioned. It tempts you to question God's care. But, I connected with God's love, and I am now persuaded in the fact that nothing shall separate us from the love of God which is in Christ Jesus. Not even sickness, pain and suffering. God loved me in the midst of my pain.

ACKNOWLEDGMENTS

I am grateful to my wife, Angela, who has been my biggest cheerleader, not just with this project, but through my health challenges that left me grappling for answers and solutions. Without her support and suggestions, this book would have never seen the light of day. Through it all, you have truly shown me what love unlimited looks like. I thank God He sent you to be my life partner!

I want to acknowledge my beloved Metropolitan New Testament Mission Baptist Church in Albany, New York, for your never-ending support. You have listened to this series on love week-after-week and have willfully accepted the challenge to display patience and kindness in your daily walk.

Thank you to my book publisher, Lisa King DeJesus, and your entire team at King Jesus Press LLC for your expertise and professionalism while bringing this book to life.

Lastly, I want to thank my DPJ Ministries Team for your support and willingness to step in wherever needed. Collectively, your efforts on this endeavor will help advance the Kingdom of God as I seek to take God's word to the masses through "Love Unlimited."

Love Unlimited

ABOUT THE AUTHOR

The Reverend Dr. Damone Paul Johnson is a recognized teacher, preacher and author. He is the senior pastor of Metropolitan New Testament Mission Baptist Church in Upstate New York. Since he began his pastoral ministry in 2003, the intergenerational congregation at Metro has grown significantly in ministry and mission. The church's footprint has expanded in its beloved community, and Dr. Johnson has shaped a virtual church ministering to people around the world weekly using Facebook, YouTube, and the church's website. He is also the founder of DPJ Ministries, whose mission is to take the word of God to the world.

Dr. Johnson is the president of the Empire Baptist Missionary Convention Congress of Christian Education, an auxiliary of the Empire Baptist Missionary Convention of New York Inc. and a proud member of Alpha Phi Alpha Fraternity, Inc., Beta Phi Lambda Chapter, where he serves as chaplain for the Eastern Region.

Dr. Johnson earned a Bachelor of Arts Degree in Religion and Philosophy with a minor in Music from Fisk University in Nashville, Tennessee, and a Master of Divinity degree from Colgate-Rochester Divinity School in Rochester, New York. In May 2007, Dr. Johnson was conferred the Doctor of Ministry degree with a concentration in Pastoral Preaching from Christian Theological Seminary in Indianapolis, Indiana. He received the distinguished Dr. H. Beecher Hicks Jr. preaching award, demonstrating strong promise in preaching and pastoral ministry.

In addition to "Love Unlimited," Dr. Johnson is the author of "Bonded Love: How God's Love Shines Through Imperfect Relationships" (the book and study guide), "A Life Worth Rebuilding," (the book and study guide) and "Beyond the Grave" Devotional.

Committed to family, Dr. Johnson is married to the love of his life, Angela Johnson.

Stay Connected!

Website: www.damonepauljohnson.com

Facebook and Instagram: @dpjministries

Email: dpjministries@gmail.com

www.ingramcontent.com/pod-product-compliance
Lightning Source LLC
Chambersburg PA
CBHW071901070526
44583CB00016B/1795